ROUTLEDGE LIBRARY EDITIONS: FINANCIAL MARKETS

Volume 6

THE ECONOMICS OF THE SWAP MARKET

THE ECONOMICS OF THE SWAP MARKET

BRENDAN BROWN

LONDON AND NEW YORK

First published in 1989 by Routledge

This edition first published in 2018
by Routledge
2 Park Square, Milton Park, Abingdon, Oxon OX14 4RN

and by Routledge
711 Third Avenue, New York, NY 10017

Routledge is an imprint of the Taylor & Francis Group, an informa business

British Library Cataloguing in Publication Data
A catalogue record for this book is available from the British Library

ISBN: 978-1-138-56537-1 (Set)
ISBN: 978-0-203-70248-2 (Set) (ebk)
ISBN: 978-1-138-56067-3 (Volume 6) (hbk)
ISBN: 978-0-203-71311-2 (Volume 6) (ebk)

Publisher's Note
The publisher has gone to great lengths to ensure the quality of this reprint but points out that some imperfections in the original copies may be apparent.

Disclaimer
The publisher has made every effort to trace copyright holders and would welcome correspondence from those they have been unable to trace.

The economics of the swap market

Brendan Brown

Routledge
London and New York

First published 1989
by Routledge
11 New Fetter Lane, London EC4P 4EE
29 West 35th Street, New York, NY 10001

© 1989 Brendan Brown
Photoset by Mayhew Typesetting, Bristol, England
Printed and bound in Great Britain
by Billing & Sons Limited, Worcester

British Library Cataloguing in Publication Data
Brown, Brendan
    The economics of the swap market.
    1. Swap markets
    I. Title
    332

    ISBN 0-415-03503-1

Library of Congress Cataloging in Publication Data
Brown, Brendan, 1951–
    The economics of the swap market/Brendan Brown.
        p. cm.
    Bibliography: p.
    Includes index.
    ISBN 0-415-03503-1
    1. Swaps (Finance) I. Title.
HG3881.B6843 1989   89-33927
332.4′5 – dc20   CIP

To Lorraine and Judith

and to my mother, Irene Brown

Contents

Tables

Foreword

Swaps are one of the great innovations of international finance – to be put alongside forward exchange and the Euro-markets. Barely a decade ago the swap had yet to be developed, existing only in various quaint 'prehistoric' forms to be used in a few esoteric transactions. Today over 20 per cent of international bond issues are linked to swap transactions. The swap has become a commonplace tool for corporations throughout the OECD world to 'lock in' interest rates on their borrowing. Small and medium-sized corporations have unprecedented opportunities via the swap to borrow at a fixed rate of interest in a wide range of currencies.

It is hardly surprising, given the rapid development of the swap, that the economics literature has failed to keep pace. Books and articles on the new market have been concentrated in the areas of legal issues, technical practice, and the merits or otherwise of regulatory proposals. The aim of the present book is to contribute to a redressing of the balance. Subjects covered include both those conventionally falling within the scope of micro-economics (broadly chapters 1–3) and of macro-economics (chapter 4).

First, in chapter 1, the forces behind the take-off of the swap market are explored. In the process, the highlights and structure of the market place are pointed out – for example, the sources of supply and demand, how liquidity is created, how price is determined, and which institutions have a comparative advantage in acting as intermediaries. In the next chapter comes a formal setting out of key arbitrage relationships which hold in equilibrium between the swap markets and bond markets, both for one currency and for many currencies. The nearest comparison to these relationships elsewhere in economics is the statement and elaboration of the so-called interest rate parity theorem, which links interest rate differentials between currencies to forward exchange premiums and discounts.

The third chapter is concerned with the dynamics of disequilibrium. What happens when there is a disturbance in one or more of the markets tied together by the arbitrage relationships described in chapter 2? One type of disturbance is structural – for example, a long-term increase in demand for swaps, or a swing-round of the budget balance into large surplus. Structural change can have a lasting impact on the normal differentials between swap rates and spreads of Euro-bond yields over government bond yields in various currencies. Examples are drawn from contemporary history.

Finally, in the last chapter, the influence of swap markets on international capital flows is described. It is shown how swap markets have increased the sensitivity of flows to fixed-rate interest differentials. Early attempts by central banks to control this by-product of the swap were rapidly abandoned. New scope for 'zonalization' of currency choice – especially for investors and borrowers in Europe to increase the proportion of their portfolios in Deutschmarks or mark-related currencies at the expense of the dollar without sacrificing some diversification of debtor risk or paying higher costs – has been created. A 'democratization' has occurred whereby, thanks to the swap, many small and medium-sized currencies have assumed an important international investment role for the first time. Various barriers to international capital flow – including withholding taxes – have been reduced in size.

All this is not to overstate the case. The swap is not the wheel. Yet the significant cost savings which the innovation of swaps has brought for a broad range of everyday-type financial transactions, domestically and internationally, were bound to have important consequences at the level both of individual financial management and of the macro-economy. The full potential is almost certainly not yet exploited for such a recent innovation.

B.B.

Chapter one

The market place

The take-off of the swap markets into a period of rapid growth in the mid and late 1980s has some parallels with that of the Euro-markets two decades earlier. The pre-take-off period of both is now the subject of folklore. It is recounted that the Soviet Union's desire to hold dollar deposits outside the USA at the height of the Cold War gave birth to the Euro-dollar. But the later flourishing of the Euro-dollar depended on the weighty influences of US regulations, technological progress, currency liberalization in Europe, the breakdown of the Bretton Woods international monetary system, the advent of OPEC, and internationalization of investment choice.

The same distinction between forces present at creation and those behind the subsequent take-off can be made for the swap markets. According to many accounts, it was the World Bank's inability in 1982 to raise sufficient fixed-rate Swiss francs and Deutschmark funds by conventional means that gave birth to the modern swap.[1] The subsequent take-off was fuelled by the powerful combination of increased interest-rate volatility, the eruption of the international debt crisis, the virtual bankruptcy of many of the US savings and loan institutions, the emergence of Japan as the number one international investor, the liberalization of capital markets worldwide, the growing risk of US corporate names, zonalization of currency choice, technological change, and the new pervasive 'trading mentality'.

In order to understand the importance of these various factors in the development of the swap, it is helpful to study the characteristics of the market place. What are the different types of swap transaction? How are they triggered? Who are the transactors?

Who provides liquidity? How can supply and demand schedules be drawn up, and how are prices (swap rates) determined? In sum, these questions are the essence of the micro-economics of the swap market.

Basic types of swap

There are two basic types of swap – first, the interest-rate swap, which involves an exchange of liabilities in the same currency; second, the currency swap, which involves the exchange of liabilities in two different currencies. Under each basic type there are many possible variations. The simplest and most common interest-rate swap is the exchange of a fixed-rate against a floating-rate dollar liability. The most common type of currency swap is the exchange of a floating-rate liability in US dollars against a fixed-rate liability in another currency.

The simple dollar interest-rate swap is sometimes described as a vanilla swap. As an example, A., who already has a $10 million fixed-rate liability (for example a five-year note issue, on which the annual coupon is 10 per cent per annum), enters into a trans-action with B., who has a $10 million floating-rate liability out-standing (on which the interest rate is re-fixed at, say, six-monthly intervals, at a given margin above or below LIBOR (London inter-bank offered rate). A. undertakes to pay the floating interest on B.'s loan whilst simultaneously B. undertakes to pay the fixed interest on A.'s loan, give or take a small margin.

The margin will depend on the relative status of A. and B. For example, if A. is a top-rated sovereign borrower and B. a middle-ranking US corporation, A. would expect to be able to obtain a lower interest cost than B. Thus A. would agree to pay B.'s borrowing costs only if a margin were deducted from them in return for B. paying A.'s fixed-rate borrowing costs in full. Equivalently, B. might agree to pay A.'s fixed-rate costs plus a small margin in return for A. paying B.'s floating-rate costs.

In practice, for dealing purposes, vanilla-type interest-rate swaps are quoted in standardized form, where it is assumed that the floating interest rate is equal to six-month LIBOR. The swap rate is expressed as a margin above US Treasury yields, usually stated on an annualized basis. For example, a five-year swap rate of 75 points means that a borrower with a five-year floating-rate debt outstanding on which the interest cost is set at six-month LIBOR would be able to swap it into a five-year fixed-rate debt on which the annual cost (payable once a year) would be the yield on five-year US Treasuries plus 75 basis points. By the same token, ignoring for the moment dealing spreads, a borrower with a five-year fixed-rate debt outstanding, on which the interest was set at 75 points above US Treasury yields, would be able to swap this into five-year floating-rate debt on which the interest rate was equal to LIBOR.

Very often A. and B. will agree to use standard contracts based on the above type of quote, even though the terms of their debt outstanding are non-standard. For example, A.'s fixed-rate debt might have a coupon set at 50 points above the five-year US Treasury yield, whilst B. might have an interest rate on his floating-rate debt equal to LIBOR plus 20 points. Under the swap arrangement, A. would receive 75 points above the US Treasury yield from B. and pay to B. a floating rate equal to LIBOR. Thus, on a net basis, A. would have converted his fixed-rate debt into a floating-rate debt on which the cost would be 25 points below LIBOR, whilst B. would be paying a net fixed-rate cost equal to 95 points above US Treasury yields (in that the floating-rate interest received from A. would fall 20 points short of its servicing costs on the floating-rate loan).

In reality the fixed-rate debt outstanding of A. might have a market price significantly under par (as would be the case if the general level of interest rates had risen since the date of issue of the debt). For example, the debt in question might have a coupon of 9 per cent when the yield on new issues by similar borrowers is currently 9½ per cent. In that case, A. would normally enter into a swap contract based on a principal amount equal to the market value of his debt. The present value of the surplus of fixed interest received under the swap over interest payment obligations on the low-coupon debt would tend to equal the discount of its price below par.

Alternatively, the maturity date on A.'s and B.'s debt may differ. For example, A.'s fixed-rate debt outstanding may be repayable in ten years' time and B.'s floating-rate in five years' time. Then A. might decide to enter into a five-year swap, leaving his fixed-rate liability for years 5 to 10 unaffected. Or B. might be ready to enter into a ten-year swap, assuming a fixed-rate liability for five years beyond the maturity of his loan, no doubt on the consideration that he intends to renew it.

Even though the basis of swap contracts can be largely standardized as described, it may sometimes be necessary to include a special premium against risk of default if one of the two parties is of poor credit quality. For example, if A. considers that there is a significant probability of B. defaulting on his obligation under the swap contract, he would be concerned at the resulting possible loss should interest rates meanwhile have fallen. As compensation for the risk of loss he could require that B. pays him a higher fixed-rate amount than specified in the standard swap quote.

In practice a bank intermediary would usually stand between A. and B., especially in the case of one being of poor credit risk. Both A. and B. would enter into swap contracts (in opposite directions) with the bank. The credit risk premium would be collected in some form from B. by the bank. For example, the bank could quote a different swap rate to B. than to A. (the difference being more than the normal dealing spread) or B. could be charged a 'facility fee'.

The assessment of credit risk of the counterparty is considerably more important in the case of currency swaps than in that of interest-rate swaps. In the currency swap, obligations to pay interest and capital in two different currencies are swapped, and exchange rate fluctuations could impose a large loss on A. in the event of B. defaulting. For example, take a simple five-year dollar–mark currency swap in which A. swaps an outstanding fixed-rate liability in Deutschmarks for a five-year floating-rate dollar liability which B. has outstanding. If the Deutschmark were to appreciate far against the dollar and B. were meanwhile to default, A. could face an unexpected large extra obligation (suddenly finding that his 'synthetic' dollar liability was transformed back into a mark liability, and at the exchange rate current at the start of the contract, not today).

Despite the importance of credit risk assessment in currency swap transactions, currency swap quotes are made usually on a standardized basis – special charges to reflect credit risk being added by negotiation. For example a five-year mark–dollar swap quote of 10 points over five-year German government bond yields means that a five-year floating-rate dollar liability on which interest is set six-monthly at LIBOR can be exchanged for a five-year fixed-rate Deutschmark liability on which the interest rate (payable annually) is ten points higher than the yield on five-year German government bonds (Bunds).

In the currency swap contract corresponding to the above deal, A. (who has the Deutschmark debt outstanding) undertakes to pay B. at six-monthly intervals dollar interest equal to the LIBOR rate and, at maturity, to pay a lump sum in dollars equal to the loan principal (the dollar amount being fixed at the start of the swap); in return, B. promises to pay A. interest in Deutschmarks at a rate of 10 points over five-year Bund yields once a year and to pay a lump sum in marks at maturity (equal to the dollar loan principle above at the exchange rate established at the time of contract).

An important variation of the simple currency swap is the so-called LIBOR–LIBOR (or basis) swap. In this, the borrower, A., swaps a floating-rate liability in one currency for a floating-rate liability in another currency. For example, a mark–dollar LIBOR–LIBOR five-year swap quote of 12 basis points would mean that A., with a floating-rate dollar loan outstanding on which the interest rate was set at LIBOR, could exchange it for a floating-rate mark loan on which the rate would be LIBOR plus 12 points. Specifically, A. promises to pay to his swap counterparty, B., mark interest at the rate of LIBOR plus 12 basis points, and to pay a lump sum in marks at the end of five years equal to the principal, whilst B. undertakes to pay A. dollar interest at the rate of LIBOR and a lump sum at the end of five years equal to the principal in dollars.

The LIBOR–LIBOR swap is the closest relation to the traditional swap in the foreign exchange market.[2] In the traditional swap a given amount of foreign exchange is simultaneously sold spot and bought forward (or bought spot and simultaneously sold forward). An example is a six-month mark–dollar foreign exchange swap, in which $1 million is sold spot for Deutschmarks and simultaneously bought six months forward against Deutschmarks. The cash flows created by the transaction are equivalent to those that would be produced by borrowing Deutschmarks for six months, lending dollars for six months, and selling the dollar interest due (at maturity) forward six months for marks. Arbitrage ensures that supernormal profit cannot be made from creating the cash flows in one way rather than the other.

Before the innovation of the LIBOR–LIBOR swap a borrower wishing to convert a, say, $1 million two-year dollar loan (on which interest was set at LIBOR at six-monthly intervals) into a floating-rate Deutschmark loan would have entered, as a first step, into a six-month mark–dollar foreign exchange swap, selling dollars spot against marks and buying the same quantity of dollars back six months forward. The amount of dollars would have been set equal to $1 million plus the interest rate on the dollar loan at six months. At the same time as entering into the foreign exchange swap, the borrower would have bought the same quantity of dollars spot against marks. (The combination of the spot and swap foreign exchange transaction is a simple outright forward sale of marks against dollars; in practice, however, foreign exchange dealers usually form outright forward quotes, by putting together spot and swap deals.)[3] At the end of each six-month period the borrower would have rolled the maturing forward exchange contract over by entering into a new mark–dollar foreign exchange swap in similar fashion.

Demand for interest-rate swaps

There are many possible motives behind swap transactions, and they can be illustrated in the framework of supply and demand analysis. In the interest-rate swap market, the demand side consists of those transactors seeking to pay fixed-rate and receive floating-rate interest (equivalently, seeking to transform a floating-rate liability into a fixed-rate liability). The supply side consists of those transactors looking to receive fixed-rate interest and pay floating-rate.

The 'price' in the interest-rate swap market is the swap rate, expressed usually as a margin above the relevant government bond yield. For example, a price of 20 points in the five-year dollar interest-rate swap market means that in return for receiving floating-rate interest (each six months, set at LIBOR) the transactor must pay fixed-rate interest once-yearly at a rate 20 points above five-year US Treasury bond yields. The higher the price the less will be the demand for the swaps, and the greater will be the supply.

Let us look first at some typical transactions on the demand side of the market.[4] First, there are institutions who face a structural excess demand for fixed-rate finance over their own access to fixed-rate funds. For example, in the USA the savings and loan associations have large portfolios of fixed-rate mortgages, yet their deposit base is essentially floating-rate. The associations cannot feasibly obtain fixed-rate funds from the bond markets, given their poor credit rating.[5] Hence the savings and loan associations have swapped large amounts of floating-rate funds into fixed-rate. They have often had to pay a premium above the standard price quotations in view of the counterparty's concern at their risk of default.

Also banks – particularly in the USA – have faced a demand for fixed-rate loans from customers that could not be satisfied out of their sometimes limited fixed-rate deposit base. US banks – unlike, for example, German or Swiss banks – do not have a ready market among their retail clients to which they can sell their own fixed-rate notes. They can sometimes obtain fixed-rate funds from the capital market. Yet there are constraints. First, many US banks, even where a bond issue is feasible, would have to pay a high rate, given their poor credit quality. Second, even when their credit rating is respectable, the yield on their notes would have to reflect the risk of the bank's profit stream to a greater extent than the rate of interest on deposits (including fixed rates on long-term deposits and on retail-type notes), which have 'first claim' on the banks' assets and are likely to be lifeboated by the government in the event of a crisis. Thus US banks have been important on the demand side of the US swap market.

Many corporations are in a position to obtain fixed-rate funds other than directly from a bank. For example, they can issue bonds themselves. Or they can enter a swap deal, transforming their floating-rate bank loan into a fixed-rate loan. In practice, a wide range of corporations are large enough to transact directly in the swap market at near wholesale rates whilst not well enough known to the non-bank public to issue bonds on acceptable terms. Such corporations may well see advantage in pursuing the swap route to fixed-rate funds.

As illustration, a corporation might be unwilling to pay an extra cost for a long-maturity rather than a short-maturity (roll-over) loan from its bank, preferring to proceed on the view that its profit performance will be sufficient to obtain a roll-over of short-term funds on equal or better terms to the present. And the bank, if it has no natural source of fixed-rate funds, might prefer in any case to lend on a roll-over basis, offering its services simultaneously as a swap market broker. Perhaps, via its interbank relationships, the bank will have ready access to a supply of swaps from other banks which have a natural source of fixed-rate funds but few natural commercial outlets. These latter banks may themselves be unwilling to make long-term loans in the interbank markets, preferring the liquidity and safety of short-term placements, cancelling exposure to interest-rate risk by entering the swap market (as a fixed-rate receiver, floating-rate payer).

Another advantage of the swap route to fixed-rate finance, from the viewpoint of both banks and corporations, is its flexibility. Many borrowers are uncertain of the amount or duration of finance which they will require. Fixed-rate loans are usually not repayable, either wholly or partly, at short notice – or redeemable from a late intermediate date (say, from two years onwards). Floating-rate loans are more flexible, as banks are able to fund fluctuations in their floating-rate loan books at very short notice in the highly liquid interbank markets. Hence flexible fixed-rate financing is most cheaply obtained by combining floating-rate borrowing with a swap transaction.

The flexibility of the swap route is also important to those borrowers who could readily obtain funds from the bond market, albeit there is often a cost attached. A top borrower would normally 'lock-in' a cheaper fixed-rate cost of finance by making a straight debt issue rather than by hedging floating-rate bank credit in the swap market. Such borrowers – like the lesser-known ones – can also use swaps to take views relatively cheaply on interest rate trends.

For example, a borrower who fears a much larger rise in interest rates over the next two years than discounted in the market might hedge his exposure by entering into a two-year interest-rate swap (as a fixed-rate payer, floating-rate receiver). True, he could alternatively have hedged his exposure in the interest-rate futures market – but the transaction cost of arranging the three-month positions there could be considerable and there would be the inconvenience of margin requirements, margin calls, and visibility. (If interest rates do not rise as the speculator expects, his futures position shows a visible loss; by contrast, the 'opportunity loss' of having swapped floating-rate into fixed-rate funds can be hidden.)

In principle, investors, like borrowers, could take views on interest rate trends by entering into swap transactions. For example, an investor with a portfolio of fixed-rate bonds could hedge his exposure against a rise in interest rates by becoming a fixed-rate receiver. Given, however, the low transaction costs in most bond markets, it could be cheaper in general simply to liquidate a proportion of the bond portfolio and move into cash.

None the less, investors are active on the demand side of the swap market, but as arbitragers, not as speculators. Specifically, investment banks have developed a so-called 'asset packaging' business. The business usually involves selling to investors 'synthetic' floating-rate notes, created by packaging a fixed-rate bond together with a swap contract (in which the investor would be a fixed-rate payer and a floating-rate receiver). Success in the business usually depends on the packager identifying 'cheap' fixed-rate bonds in the secondary market, and having access to investor clients interested in floating-rate assets even if somewhat less liquid than mainstream forms.

For example, Japanese financial institutions have had a considerable appetite for floating-rate assets showing a return above LIBOR (their own cost of funding). They have been unwilling to obtain these by making direct loans (which would be illiquid). Yet the high-quality floating-rate notes and commercial paper which enjoy liquid markets have offered returns only well below LIBOR rates. Asset packagers have filled the gap in the market by presenting combinations of, say, A-rated bonds on which the yield is far above the relevant Treasury yield, and a swap.

The arithmetic of the asset package could be roughly as follows. A single-A US five-year corporate bond is showing a yield of 85 points above the five-year US Treasury bond. The five-year swap rate is 70 points. Hence the investor who simultaneously purchases the given corporate bond and enters into the swap transaction as a fixed-rate payer will end up with a synthetic floating-rate note yielding 15 points above LIBOR. The package will not be illiquid, in that the swap could be reversed, albeit at some cost (possibly by entering into a swap in the opposite direction for a similar maturity – most swap dealers are ready to quote rates, albeit not the finest, for non-standard maturity dates), whilst the fixed-rate bond can be sold in the secondary market (again, liquidity here may be far from perfect).

It may be asked why the given corporation should make a fixed-rate bond issue if substantial demand exists for its paper in floating-rate form. Surely it would do better by itself issuing floating-rate paper and entering into one big swap (paying fixed, receiving floating interest)? Both the investor and borrower should gain from the saving of transaction cost involved by consolidating lots of small swap transactions into one large one and from the greater liquidity created for the investor (in that he no longer has to liquidate a swap position in the event of sale).

It is possible, however, that market conditions for the corporation's debt have changed since the date of issue. The debt, whilst originally issued at a price where asset-swapping was unattractive, may now have moved to a cheaper level – perhaps reflecting a deterioration in its credit quality, or perhaps reflecting a temporary large amount on offer in the secondary market from an investor seeking cash. (Asset swaps can add to the liquidity of the secondary market in fixed-rate bonds by allowing paper to be disposed of to investors seeking floating-rate as well as to those seeking fixed-rate paper.)

In addition, even at the point of new issue, the borrower seeking fixed-rate finance may derive advantage from targeting a proportion of his notes at asset swappers (investors interested in floating-rate placement via asset swaps). For example, a corporation of single-A rating might find that, at the yield at which it can issue fixed-rate bonds, investors would be able to package these (via asset swaps) into synthetic floating-rate notes offering a significant margin over LIBOR. Yet there may also exist substantial demand for its paper in fixed-rate form (among investors looking for a higher yield than obtainable on prime paper).

Calculation may show that fixed-rate funds can be obtained more cheaply by aiming an issue at both types of investor, those looking for fixed-rate paper and those interested in floating-rate paper (including in synthetic form), rather than by issuing floating-rate paper (at a margin above LIBOR sufficient to sell the lot to floating-rate investors). One factor in the calculation is sometimes the ability of the investment bank launching the issue to place a substantial proportion of the issue at an above-market price with captive retail clients (who would not be interested in floating-rate paper).

Investment banks are sometimes active on the demand side of the interest-rate swap market on their own account as well as on behalf of their customers. For example, the investment bank may be launching a large fixed-rate issue for a top borrower in the Euro-dollar bond market. Until the paper has been sold, it is held by the bank, which is thereby exposed to a rise in Euro-dollar bond yields. The bank could hedge its risk by entering into an interest-rate swap, for the same maturity as the bond, as a fixed-rate payer and floating-rate receiver. The inventory of unsold notes would be financed on a floating-rate basis.

In practice, investment banks hedge issues more often in the US Treasury sale-and-repurchase market (buying Treasury bonds spot and simultaneously selling them forward), selling the bonds delivered under the sale-and-repurchase agreement spot for cash. The attraction of this procedure is its low cost, reflecting the considerable liquidity of the sale-and-repurchase market. Yet the swap route to hedging provides a more complete hedge, in that swap rates are more highly correlated than the US Treasury yields with Euro-dollar bond yields. (The high correlation stems from the various arbitrage relationships between the Euro-bond and swap markets described in the next chapter.)

Investment banks sometimes enter the swap market on a purely speculative basis – to take a view on the movement of the swap rate. For example, if the bank believes that five-year swap rates are going to rise over the next year by more than what is already discounted in the swap yield curve (the difference between six-year and one-year swap rates), it could profitably enter the six-year swap market as a fixed-rate payer whilst entering the one-year swap market as a fixed-rate receiver. At the end of year 1 the bank would expect to liquidate the long-term contract by entering into a five-year swap as a fixed-rate receiver.

Supply of interest-rate swaps

The single most important source of supply of interest-rate swaps (fixed-rate receivers, floating-rate payers) are top-quality issuers of fixed-rate Euro-bonds. They might enter the swap market on the supply side when floating-rate funds can be obtained more cheaply by combining a fixed-rate issue with a swap than directly in floating-rate form. For example, suppose the Republic of Italy could float a five-year fixed-rate Euro-dollar bond at a yield 40 basis points higher than on five-year US Treasuries, and the five-year dollar swap rate were 70 points (again measured relative to five-year Treasuries). Then, by entering the swap market as a fixed-rate receiver and floating-rate payer, Italy could obtain floating-rate dollar finance at an effective cost of 30 points below LIBOR.

Suppose that cost is less than the rate Italy would have to offer on a five-year floating note issue and less than the cost of alternative types of floating-rate finance (where an adjustment may have to be made for the fact that some types – for example, commercial paper – have to be rolled over at frequent intervals at uncertain margins relative to LIBOR or other benchmarks). Then Italy, in so far as it sought floating-rate dollar funds, would be a source of supply in the dollar interest-rate swap market.

The less prime the borrower the less probable is it that combining a swap with a fixed-rate issue will prove to be a cheap route to floating-rate finance (see chapter 3, p. 60). None the less, the non-prime borrower will sometimes be on the supply side of the swap market, but not generally in the role of arbitrager. He may, for example, believe that interest rates are about to fall sharply, and wish to transform thereby fixed-rate liabilities into floating. Or he may wish to 'lock-in' a profit on fixed-rate liabilities entered into when interest rates were much lower.

Also the investor can be found on the supply side of the interest-rate swap market, but not to the same extent as on the demand side. For example, an investor might see holding a portfolio of highly liquid short-term dollar paper combined with a swap position in which he is a fixed-rate receiver and floating-rate payer as an attractive way of obtaining a yield close to that on a portfolio of AA-rated Euro-dollar bonds and yet at a higher level of liquidity (in that one large swap transaction could be reversed more cheaply than liquidating a whole portfolio or less-than-prime Euro-dollar bonds).

In principle, asset packaging could generate a supply of interest-rate swaps. The packaging would be different in nature from that involved in the production of synthetic floating-rate notes and which is one source of demand in the interest-rate swap market. On the supply side, packaging would take the form of buying floating-rate notes and combining them with a swap (pay floating-rate, receive fixed-rate) to produce a synthetic fixed-rate note. Such packaging is not normally feasible with respect to prime issues, as they are in scarce supply (given the considerable scope for prime borrowers to obtain cheap floating-rate funds via fixed-rate issues combined with a swap).

In practice, asset packaging in the floating-rate note market is mainly concerned with issues of less-than-prime borrowers. The issues were usually aimed, at the time of launch, at banks, who would be attracted by their potential liquidity advantage over conventional loans. Non-banks would in general not have sufficient credit-rating information to allow them to be active investors in such paper. Even so, some non-banks, including institutional investors, are interested in the less-than-prime names – both in floating-rate form and in repackaged form as synthetic high-yielding fixed-rate bonds. In the latter role they are on the supply side of the interest-rate swap market.

A 'supply-sider' – of much greater importance – is the arbitrager between the new issue market, the interest-rate swap markets, and the currency swap markets. In the dollar interest-rate swap market, for example, supply often comes from borrowers ultimately seeking finance in another currency. The keen demand for interest-rate swaps in dollars – reflecting their widespread use by middle corporate America and by the mortgage industry – means that it is sometimes cheaper for a top international borrower seeking, say, fixed-rate Deutschmark finance, to obtain it indirectly by, first, issuing a fixed-rate Euro-dollar bond, second, entering into a dollar interest-rate swap as a fixed-rate receiver and floating-rate payer, and, third, entering into a dollar–mark currency swap as a receiver of floating-rate dollars and a payer of fixed-rate marks.

Supply and demand of currency swaps

In the most liquid currency swap markets – those in which six-month LIBOR in dollars is the benchmark for the floating-rate obligation – the consistent practice with the interest-rate swap market in dollars is to describe the would-be fixed-rate payers of foreign currency and receivers of floating-rate dollars as on the demand side, and would-be fixed-rate receivers of foreign currency and payers of floating-rate dollars as on the supply side. In practice, a large share of both supply and demand in these dollar LIBOR-based currency swap markets stems from dealers putting together non-dollar swaps (for example, fixed-rate marks into fixed-rate francs). Hence a wider span of analysis than just the dollar-based market place is required to understand the rationale behind many currency swaps.

None the less, there are important categories of client business in the currency swap markets between floating-rate dollars and fixed rates in other currencies. For example, a supranational borrower seeking floating-rate finance in dollars might find that the cheapest source involves issuing a Euro-sterling bond, then entering into a pound–dollar currency swap (in which the supranational would be a receiver of fixed-rate sterling and a payer of floating-rate dollars). Behind this swap opportunity could be strong international demand for Euro-sterling bonds, or strong demand for fixed-rate sterling in the pound swap markets, or some combination of the two.

One source of demand in the pound–dollar swap market is borrowers who have already established keenly priced lines of credit on floating-rate dollars and who find that they have a requirement for fixed-rate sterling finance (perhaps to hedge a long-run fixed income stream expected in sterling). A second source is banks active in the Euro-dollar deposit market who are seeking to fund fixed-rate lending in sterling (perhaps related to long-term trade financing). A third source is arbitrage demand originating from the interest-rate swap market. For example, a corporation might find that it is cheaper to obtain fixed-rate pounds by borrowing floating-rate dollars and entering into a pound–dollar currency swap than by borrowing floating-rate pounds and entering into a pound interest-rate swap.

Dealers themselves are of course keen to spot opportunities for arbitrage between the interest-rate and currency swap markets. Often this will involve them transacting in the LIBOR–LIBOR (sometimes called 'basis') swap market. For example, as an alternative to taking on a position in the pound interest-rate swap market as a fixed-rate payer, the dealer might find that it is cheaper to combine a transaction in the pound–dollar currency swap market (as a fixed-rate payer of pounds, receiver of floating-rate dollars) with one in the pound–dollar LIBOR–LIBOR swap market (as a payer of floating-rate dollars and receiver of floating-rate pounds).

Indeed, arbitragers between the currency swap and interest-rate swap markets play a very important role in the LIBOR–LIBOR swap markets. Other players there include arbitragers with the traditional forward exchange market. For example, a bank which has entered into a five-year dollar–mark LIBOR–LIBOR swap with a customer, in which the bank is the receiver of floating-rate marks and payer of floating-rate dollars, could square its position by selling marks six months forward against dollars (the amount of dollars purchased equal to the principal of the LIBOR–LIBOR swap plus the dollar interest due to be paid under that swap at the end of six months) and intending to roll-over the maturing forward contract into a similar new contract (adjusted in dollar amount for any change in the dollar LIBOR rate).

Normal covered interest arbitrage between the money markets and the forward exchange market should ensure that the amount in marks due to be delivered under each forward contract approximates to the mark equivalent of the principal plus interest thereon. Hence the possibility of arbitrage between the LIBOR–LIBOR market and the forward exchange market helps to explain why LIBOR–LIBOR swap rates are very close to zero. For example, a typical LIBOR–LIBOR dollar–sterling swap quote is flat ⅛, meaning that a borrower of dollars at LIBOR could swap them into a sterling borrowing at LIBOR + ⅛, whilst a borrower of sterling at LIBOR could swap this into a dollar borrowing at LIBOR. (The difference between the two quotes represents the dealer's spread.)

An example of non-arbitrage activity in the LIBOR–LIBOR swap markets would be a borrower with a long-term floating-rate dollar loan outstanding deciding to swap this into floating-rate marks. It is true that many large-scale borrowings have a so-called multi-currency option facility, whereby the borrower at the end of each six-month period can repay the original loan and draw down the equivalent amount in another nominated currency. But, should the chosen currency appreciate far against the original, the borrower may find that he runs up against his loan ceiling (fixed in the original currency) and be forced to make some early repayment. The borrower would avoid cash-flow uncertainty during the lifetime of the loan by entering instead into a LIBOR–LIBOR swap.

Another example is where a bank finds that in one currency its natural deposit base exceeds the likely demand for floating-rate loans from clients, whilst in another currency the asymmetry is in the reverse direction. The bank may find it cheaper to balance its books in the two currencies by transacting in the LIBOR–LIBOR swap market than relying on operations in the traditional forward exchange market (or in the conventional currency swap market).

LIBOR–LIBOR swap business, in contrast to other currency swap business, almost always involves the dollar on one side of the transaction. The most common examples of non-dollar business in the wider market place is between Swiss francs and Deutschmarks, Swiss francs and Japanese yen, and French francs and Deutschmarks. Sometimes such swaps are negotiated (via an intermediary) directly between two fixed-rate borrowers rather than involving the 'pivot' of a floating-rate debt. Direct swaps between two fixed-rate debts (in different currencies) are also found in deals involving the dollar.

As illustration, some German banks have found that they can issue bonds in the Swiss market on particularly favourable terms (presumably on account of the popularity of their paper among Swiss investors). Hence they have derived cheap fixed-rate funding in marks by issuing fixed-rate bonds in Switzerland and swapping into fixed-rate marks. The counterpart in the swap could be, for example, a German corporation seeking fixed-rate Swiss franc financing for an investment in Switzerland or simply willing to take a speculative view that the interest rate saving on francs *vis-à-vis* marks will be greater than any exchange rate loss (inflicted by the franc rising against the mark).

The Swiss franc–yen swap market has been active owing to the popularity of the Swiss note market among Japanese borrowers. Many less well known Japanese corporations have been attracted to the private placement market in Switzerland. Swiss bankers have cultivated a keen appetite among their clients for Japanese private placements (for which the prospectus requirements are less onerous than in many other markets), often offering the sweetener of an equity option attached to the debt. In turn the Japanese borrowers have in some cases looked to swap the fixed-rate francs obtained into fixed-rate yen. The counterparty to the swap is sometimes another Japanese corporation wishing to increase its liabilities in francs, perhaps on the view that there is little prospect of franc appreciation against the yen and so the interest cost saving (on francs *vis-à-vis* yen) is genuine. Alternatively a pair of indirect counterparties involving a third currency could be found, for example, in the form of a non-Japanese issuer of Euro-yen bonds wishing to swap into his base currency and another borrower wanting to swap from that base currency into fixed-rate francs, perhaps on an exchange rate view.

Indeed, the importance of speculation on exchange rate movement should not be underestimated as a factor in generating currency swap business. Before the innovation of swaps, borrowers who raised finance in a foreign currency were committed to taking a fairly long-term view on exchange rate movement. True, they could reduce their exposure to the foreign currency by building up assets in it – but that might be an inefficient use of their capital resources – or by taking positions in the forward exchange market – but that could involve significant transaction costs on roll-over dates and large variations in cash flow (and in recorded profits based on accounting conventions). Occasionally they could call the foreign currency debt for early redemption[6] – but that could involve substantial costs, not least in reissuing new debt in another market.

By entering into a currency swap, in contrast, the borrower can change the currency exposure of his long-term debt at frequent intervals and at low cost based on short-term exchange rate views. The swap salesman looking to find a counterparty, for example, to the World Bank swapping from dollars into Deutschmarks (a transaction which has been common for the World Bank in the past, when it was keen to obtain finance in low-interest-rate marks, yet the appetite of the German bond market for its paper – at prime rates – was limited) would identify international borrowers with Deutschmark debt outstanding who might be keen to alter their currency exposure.

The creation of liquidity

There are two main agents responsible for liquidity creation in markets[7] – the market-maker and the broker. The market-maker stands ready to buy or sell at his quoted bid or offer rates any amount (up to a conventionally set limit) of the given commodity (including financial products). His profit is derived from the bid–offer spread, against which must be set his running operational costs and net losses made from adverse market movements on his holding of inventory (which may be positive or – as in the case of a short position – negative). The broker, by contrast, does not deal on his own account, but seeks to match buyers and sellers. Brokers, unlike market-makers, do not offer instantaneous liquidity.

17

In some markets the market-maker is the predominant agent of liquidity creation – for example, in foreign exchange, bill, and bond markets, a high volume of market turnover, a low level of price volatility, a wholly standardized commodity, and a low capital requirement, all help to promote the business of market-making. In other markets the market-maker is wholly absent. For example, in the real estate market, liquidity depends wholly on brokers; market-making is infeasible in view of the highly non-standardized product, the impossibility of 'going short' (whereby the dealer could deliver a house which he did not own), and the largely unknown – and in many cases poor – credit status of buyers and sellers.

Swap markets – like real estate markets – depend essentially on brokers for their liquidity. The swap brokers (including investment banks acting in this role), however, are ready sometimes to deal on their own account, albeit on a discretionary basis, (there is no firm commitment to buy and sell at their two-way prices; such quotes are only 'indications' of the price at which the broker would expect to be able eventually to conclude the deal). Hence the swap market lies closer in the spectrum of liquidity to the securities and foreign exchange market than to the real estate market.

Handicaps encountered by the potential market-maker in swaps include, first, the heterogeneity of the product. One element in the heterogeneity is the credit profile of the parties. For example, an interest-rate swap in which the proposed counterparty is an AAA-rated borrower is significantly different from one in which the counterparty is a BBB corporation. The would-be receiver of fixed-rate (and payer of floating-rate) interest would require a higher swap rate (fixed-rate payment relative to LIBOR) from the BBB than from the AAA counterparty.

Another element in the heterogeneity is maturity dates. For example, the broker might have to wait a long time to match a would-be fixed-rate payer (in a dollar interest-rate swap) for six years with a would-be fixed-rate receiver for the same period. Instead, for a price, he might be willing to assume the mismatch in maturity himself, receiving fixed-rate interest under a six-year swap contract entered into with A., whilst paying fixed-rate interest under a five-year swap contract entered into with B. The broker's customer might be willing to accept a somewhat less keen quote than normal in order to achieve speedy conclusion of a deal in this form. The broker (assumed to be an investment bank in this case) would have to calculate a 'price' which justified accepting the implicit risk exposure and adjust his quote correspondingly.

A second handicap to market-making in swaps is the amount of risk involved in inter-market-maker business. Such business is crucial to market-making. For example, in the spot foreign exchange market a bank can close a position resulting from a client transaction (say, short of the dollar and long in marks) by dealing with another bank which has an opposite position (probably resulting from this second bank buying dollars against the marks), and assumes very limited credit exposure thereby (limited because settlement is only two days ahead, and the credit status of the counterpart bank is unlikely to change during that time). The facility of offsetting positions with other market-makers means that these can be closed much more rapidly than if the bank had to wait for a second client wishing to deal in the opposite direction – hence the average exposure to foreign risk in market-making for clients is reduced, meaning that narrower bid–offer spreads (than otherwise) can be quoted.

In the swap markets, inter-market-maker business would involve the parties having credit-risk exposure to each other extending often over a period of many years. Hence investment banks active in swaps tend to limit strictly the extent to which they deal with other banks in managing their 'book'. For example, a bank which has entered into a dollar interest-rate swap with a client would hope to offset the position with another client deal rather than with another bank; if, instead, it routinely offset positions with other banks, the number of swap contracts into which it would enter to serve a given amount of customer business would be much greater, and so would the amount of credit risk which it incurred.

Clients, realizing the obstacles in the way of banks 'offloading' positions in the swap market and the disadvantageous price (swap rate) they (the client) would obtain if they insisted on an immediate binding quote, are usually prepared to use the bank as a broker, giving it some time to match a client in the opposite direction. None the less, the bank's role usually extends beyond that of simple broker to actually becoming a party to a swap contract with each client (in opposite directions). Most clients are not in a position to make credit-risk assessments and pricing calculations for non-bank counterparties found by the bank – nor would they blandly accept the bank's assessment as a basis for entering into a direct contract. The exception is where the bank can locate two clients (wishing to deal in opposite directions) who are of prime credit status – indeed, of higher status than the bank itself. (In that case it would be inefficient for the bank to stand as contact intermediary, causing both parties to accept greater credit risk than if they concluded a contract directly with each other.)

The bank's role as a contract party in most of the swap deals which it effects, together with the long-term nature of the contracts (and their risk), all lie behind the relative capital intensity of liquidity creation in the swap market. Even so, the bank has considerable scope to hold that capital intensity in check, whilst still providing a dealing quote quite speedily to clients, by transacting in allied liquid markets to reduce risk.

For example, the bank, having entered into a five-year interest-rate swap contract with client A., whereby it (the bank) receives fixed-rate and pays floating, without yet having located another client wishing to assume a position in the opposite direction, can contain its risk exposure in the interim by taking a short position in five-year US Treasury bonds. The short position would be achieved normally by operating first in the sale-and-repurchase market for US Treasuries (effectively a market for short-term lending and borrowing on a secured basis – the security being US Treasury bonds) – selling five-year US Treasury bonds forward, say, for one week, and simultaneously buying the bonds spot. Second, the bonds acquired under the sale-and-repurchase agreement would be sold spot. Once the bank had found a client as a swap counterparty it would unwind this hedge.

The hedge is not perfect. The principle residual risk is that the swap rate (expressed as a margin above the five-year Treasury bond yield) will rise before the counterparty is found. In addition, there is the less important mismatch between the bank's liability to pay a fixed-interest amount (set at LIBOR) at the end of the first six months and the uncertain amount of interest which the bank will accumulate after the liquidation (or maturing) of the sale-and-repurchase agreement.

Even so, hedging opportunities in the dollar interest-rate swap markets are in general superior to those in others. In particular, the cost of going short in government bond markets outside the USA is significant. Even where futures markets exist in government bonds, the contracts are for a standard maturity which frequently will not coincide with that of the swap position. The difficulty of hedging non-dollar interest-rate swap positions is in turn a handicap to liquidity in the currency swap market.

For example, consider the position of a bank which has entered into a Deutschmark–dollar currency swap with a client whereby the bank is a fixed-rate receiver of Deutschmarks and a floating-rate payer of US dollars (say, over a five-year period). One way in which the bank in principle could hedge a substantial part of the exposure (in the interim until another client is found as counter-party) would be to short-sell a five-year German government bond (Bund), sell the proceeds spot for US dollars, and lend these in the six-month Euro-dollar market.

In practice, the cost of running a short position in Bunds may be such as to make any quote, not based on a firm counterparty first being found, highly unattractive. The bank will consider the possibility not just of one direct counterparty but of several indirect ones. For example, its position (as a fixed-rate Deutschmark receiver, floating-rate dollar payer) could be offset by entering into a mark interest-rate swap with client A. (whereby the bank receives floating-rate and pays fixed-rate) and a LIBOR–LIBOR swap with Client B. (whereby the bank pays floating-rate marks and receives floating-rate dollars).

Alternatively the bank could enter into a series of long-term forward exchange contracts with a range of clients whereby the bank would sell marks forward against dollars one year, two years, three years, four years, and five years – the largest deal by far being the last, which would be for an amount equal to the Deutschmark principal. These transactions would leave the bank with a five-year floating-rate dollar liability and an incoming dollar cash flow of moderately diminishing amounts at the end of years 1 to 4 (on the assumption that the forward exchange market discounts a trend appreciation of the mark against the dollar) and a big dollar inflow at the end of year 5 – larger in size than the principal of the dollar liability (again assuming the mark is at a forward premium to the dollar). The dollar inflows in years 1 to 4, by contrast, would usually be smaller than the interest due on the floating rate liability, given that the level of interest rates on marks is generally lower than on dollars.

In sum, the bank would have a floating-rate dollar liability matched by a low-coupon dollar asset (on which the coupon is not equal on each payment date but tends downwards). Though the principal amount (the nominal amount due at maturity) of the asset would exceed that of the liability, the discrepancy would largely be eliminated when both were expressed in present-value terms (in that the market value of a low-coupon bond is substantially below par). The bank could close most of the remaining exposure to interest-rate risk by entering into a dollar interest-rate swap with a further client (whereby the bank pays fixed-rate and receives floating-rate – the principal amount of the swap contract being set equal to that of the floating-rate liability).

The bank must judge on a case-by-case basis whether the likely profit on this combination of deals exceeds that on other possible combinations, and if so, whether the difference is enough to merit the greater residual risk assumed. Usually the different combinations are not simultaneously available, and the bank has to decide whether to choose speedy execution – thereby securing the business – at the cost of possibly greater profit if it could keep the would-be swap client waiting longer.

Indeed, it is in the interest of quick execution that banks active in swaps between two non-dollar currencies will often turn to a combination of two or more client deals involving the dollar to offset the originating deal. For example, having been approached by client A, who wants to pay fixed-rate Swiss francs and receive fixed-rate marks, the bank could more often offset this with a dollar–Swiss franc and dollar–mark deal than with one direct deal, in that there is a greater volume of business in both of these than between francs and marks. In turn the client found in dollar–marks, for example, may be combining that swap with one in dollar–yen to achieve a fixed-rate yen into fixed-rate mark swap. In sum, the dollar could be described as the 'entrepot' currency of the swap markets – a similar role to that which it plays in the foreign exchange markets.

In the locating of possible clients to match an originating piece of swap business (often not yet concluded) the bank will sometimes use specialist firms of brokers (these latter perform a pure broking function and do not enter into the swap contract themselves). In general, however, the brokers signal bids and offers from other banks rather than from potential non-bank clients. The latter are likely to be well serviced by several banks and would see little need to use the services of a broker. Hence, in line with the general principle of containing the extent to which swap positions are offset simply with other banks, the bank must not see the broker as the first port of call. More use could be made of brokers if banks were ready to 'hand over' clients to each other towards matching positions (rather than an additional interbank position being involved), but this would jeopardize often long-run client relationships.

Banks which are best placed to earn profits in the swap business are those which are active both in fixed-rate lending and in making new issues of fixed-rate bonds (for clients). They have two streams of clients to match against each other (bond issuers wishing to swap into floating-rate finance, and loan customers wishing to lock in fixed-rates) without having to resort to the broker network or having to pyramid interbank transactions on each originating deal. In currency swaps it is also helpful for the bank to be active in long-term forward exchange – in that the scope is thereby increased for laying-off positions cheaply (with a forward exchange client).

In sum, swap business is an important area of synergy between investment and commercial banking. This synergy could, indeed, be the main justification for investment banks and commercial banks 'operating under the same roof'. (An alternative justification would be where the commercial bank has an identified network of retail clients who are ready buyers of bond issues launched by the investment bank – the situation enjoyed by Swiss and German 'universal' banks.) Potential synergy extends beyond the swap business. Just as the latter gains from the bank being active in fixed-rate lending and bond issues, so do the latter two activities gain from the bank having a capacity to do business in swaps. In fact swap business, fixed-rate lending, and new bond issue business all thrive on each other.

In particular, a bank which is active in making fixed-rate loans to clients and has a well developed swap operation is well placed to lead fixed-rate bond issues. Whereas a pure investment bank might be justly cautious about promising a potential issuer that it could achieve say 50 points below LIBOR (by taking a gamble that a favourable swap could be arranged), the universal bank with a 'soft market' for fixed-rate loans among medium-sized corporations and house buyers could proceed more deliberately. It could

23

fix the swap rate with the commercial loan department at the time of issue, and the latter could use this rate as the benchmark for arranging fixed-rate loans in coming weeks (hedging fluctuations in market rates before borrowers were found by buying fixed-rate bonds). Sometimes, to win relationships on the bond issue side of the business, the loan department might be prevailed upon to accept a somewhat above-market benchmark rate on the swap, on the expectation that non-price-sensitive clients could be found over the medium term.

Conversely the loan department can operate with greater boldness in promoting fixed rate lending when it is well backed by a new issue and swap business elsewhere in the bank. For example, a new issue swapped (by the borrower) into floating-rate finance – the counterpart being the bank's swap department – can be the springboard to an intensive marketing effort. The loan department, knowing that substantial funds are available at the fixed rate set in the swap deal, can proceed to sell aggressively, not having to fear that they will be unable to deliver the goods. Thus a swap and new issue business can make good the lack of a retail market for bank fixed-rate notes (from the viewpoint of the loan department).

Swap origins revisited

In practice, in the very competitive market conditions of the late 1980s, banks have been cautious about going full steam ahead in the full exploitation of running swap, bond issue, and fixed-rate lending business alongside. Over-capacity in the new issue markets means that most business there has been at a loss. Commercial banks, their balance sheets already burdened in many cases by loan portfolios of dubious quality, have lacked the financial muscle to build a new venture where there is little prospect of short-term profit. There have been 'cultural differences' between commercial and investment bankers that have stood in the way of efficient communication between bond new issue departments and commercial lending departments.

Financial weakness in the banking industry has not been overall a handicap to swap market development. Indeed, the Latin America debt crisis of 1982 was a fillip to swap market activity. We will look at this example in now drawing together a synopsis of the main factors behind the take-off of the swap market.

First, there was the 'Volcker shock' of the early 1980s, when short-term US money market rates approached 20 per cent per annum. Many corporate treasurers reacted to the shock by taking the view that they should reduce their exposure to interest-rate volatility in the future. Some decided that they should also 'manage' their liabilities more actively (by timely switching between fixed rate and floating rate). Conventional sources of fixed-rate finance – the public bond markets and long-term bank loans – were in many cases effectively closed to them. The smaller corporation never had the option of public debt issues (given the unfamiliarity of its name to the public, and the potential illiquidity of a small issue), whilst even large corporations came under the growing cloud of US take-over mania. Their treasurers were reluctant to issue debt at the premium yield required to compensate investors against the risk that today's AAA paper could become tomorrow's junk bond.

In principle, banks could have met the demand for increased fixed-rate financing from the corporate sector. But in many cases their own credit rating had become impaired by the international debt crisis, limiting their access to long-term fixed-rate funds (at anything near prime rates). Moreover, in the USA and UK, banks have no well developed retail client base for fixed-rate notes (as in Germany or Switzerland) and the costs of using intermediaries to market large amounts of paper to finance fixed-rate lending could have been substantial.

Hence US corporates turned to the interest-rate swap as their preferred long-run tool for hedging interest-rate risk (as against the sometimes used short-run tool of interest-rate futures). Swaps had, in addition, the attraction of flexibility. They could be 'taken out' and 'closed' much more cheaply than publicly issued bonds. Moreover the US savings and loan associations – given doubts about their solvency – could not have raised long-term fixed-rate finance either from their client base or from the market.

In themselves these new sources of demand for swaps 'provoked' new sources of supply (where 'demand' is categorized as would-be fixed-rate payers and floating-rate receivers) in that high swap margins helped to make it feasible for some borrowers in the fixed-rate bond market – especially those that commanded any 'premium' there relative to what they would obtain in the markets for floating-rate finance – to use new issues of fixed-rate paper as a first stepping stone to cheap floating-rate funds, the second step being the conclusion of a swap transaction (as fixed-rate receiver, floating-rate payer).

In fact the eruption of the Latin American debt crisis in 1982 – and later of the Crash of 1987 – caused the above 'premium' to increase for top-quality borrowers, especially those able to make 'jumbo' issues. As investors put an increased emphasis on liquidity, jumbos rose in popularity. Furthermore, prime borrowers found it harder to justify tapping floating-rate sources of finance directly – in that one source, banks, were generally of poorer quality than themselves (and hence could not offer funds at a rate appropriate to the prime borrower's ranking, given that it did not make sense to lend at rates below their own cost of funds); whilst the other source, the primary market in floating-rate notes, had shrunk considerably. Investors, no longer facing the scare of double-digit inflation (as in the heyday of the floating-rate note market in the early 1980s) had scaled back the target proportion for floating-rate assets in their portfolios to a point where this could be largely filled by preferred short-maturity instruments – bank deposits, bills, and commercial paper.

Another stimulus to swaps from the side of supply – in this case to cross-currency business – has come from the Japanese in their new role as number one international investor. Their keen demand for high-coupon bonds even in minor currencies has created arbitrage opportunities for prime international borrowers in the form of issuing these as a first stage – the second being a currency swap (for example, receiving fixed-rate Australian dollars, paying floating-rate US dollars) – towards cheap floating-rate finance in another currency. Such arbitrage has been facilitated by a keen demand for swaps (fixed-rate payers) in the minor currency in question.

Also promoting cross-currency swap business has been the zonalization of currency choice (meaning the growing trend for investors and borrowers to seek to raise the proportion of their portfolio denominated in currencies which belong to their 'home' zone – for example, European investors raising the proportion in Deutschmark-zone currencies and reducing the share of the dollar) – itself stimulated by the evidence accumulated of dollar instability. Investors have been keen to obtain a wide diversification of credit risks in their portfolio – more extensive than if the range of names were restricted to those which had a natural demand for finance in currencies belonging to the zone in question. The 'outsiders' have been induced to satisfy investor demand by a favourable movement of currency swap rates (making it possible sometimes, for example, for a 'natural' dollar borrower to find it cheaper to issue Deutschmark paper and swap this into dollars). The counterparty to the swap is often an outside borrower (for example, a European borrower exploiting the scarcity of its name in the dollar sector to make a keenly priced issue there and swap it into cheap Deutschmark-zone finance).

As the range and variety of swaps have increased, so has their demand on technology. Programs have been devised, for example, to assess risk and possible returns on mismatched swap books, or on capital employed in arbitrage between swap and other markets. The micro-computer has doubtless lowered the potential cost of swap-making. It is far, however, from being the essential precondition for the innovation.

Chapter two

Arbitrage statics

The evolution of the forward exchange market – from its beginnings in Vienna during the 1880s to its period of rapid growth in the early interwar years – went hand in hand with a growing economics literature on its workings.[1] This culminated in the enunciation of the so-called interest-rate parity theorem, which set out the equilibrium relationship between the forward exchange rate, the spot exchange rate, and interest-rate differentials between currencies.[2] A static and dynamic version of the theorem was subsequently developed.[3] Finally, in the post-war years, the theorem has been considerably elaborated – taking account, for example, of transaction costs, the distinction between Euro and domestic money markets, political risks, and the relation of the conventional foreign exchange swap market to the outright forward exchange market.[4]

A new literature – largely written by practitioners – has likewise accompanied the take-off of the swap markets. As yet, however, there has been no clear statement of the equivalent of the interest-rate parity theorem, even though some of the equilibrium relationships between swap rates and other interest-rate and bond yield spreads are well understood in the market place. There are two basic theorems to be constructed. The first links the swap rate in the interest-rate swap market, the margin (relative to LIBOR) in the floating-rate note market, and the spread of yields in the fixed-rate Euro-bond market over yields in the government bond market all in the same currency. The second links the differential between swap rates in the interest-rate swap market in two different currencies, and the differential between Euro-bond spreads in the two respective currency sectors.

In this chapter the equilibrium relationships making up the first and second theorems are elaborated, full account being taken of real-world attributes such as transaction costs. In the next chapter, situations of disequilibrium are described, together with the forces at work which will bring a return to equilibrium. In particular, what determines the amount by which each variable adjusts to re-establish an equilibrium relationship?

The first theorem – part one

The key variable in the evaluation of a floating-rate note is the effective margin of its interest yield below LIBOR. In the case of a new issue at par, the margin is identical (from the viewpoint of the investor buying at par) to that set in the prospectus with respect to the periodic (usually six-monthly) re-fixing of the coupon. More generally, the margin must be derived from secondary market prices, taking account of the movement of money market rates since the last coupon re-fixing date.

There are four possible arbitrage transactions between the floating-rate note market, the interest-rate swap market, and the conventional fixed-rate market, which set a series of lower bounds (levels below which correcting forces are unleashed) for the margin (in the secondary market). There are a further four possible arbitrage transactions which set a series of upper bounds. To demonstrate these, the following notation is used. For simplicity of presentation, the maturity of the contracts is not specified in the notation, nor is the given debtor, but these could easily be added as subscripts or superscripts.

m is the margin by which the yield on the floating-rate note (frn) is below LIBOR as based on the bid price in the secondary market (i.e. the price relevant to the potential seller of the frn).

M is the margin by which the yield on the floating-rate note (frn) is below LIBOR as based on the offer price in the secondary market (i.e. the price relevant to the potential buyer of the frn). ($m < M$).

m' is the effective margin (including new issue costs) that the given borrower would have to offer on a new issue of a frn (where the reference is LIBOR, as for m and M above).

p is the spread of the yield on a fixed-rate bond outstanding of the given borrower above the yield on an identical maturity US Treasury bond, where the first yield is based on the offer price quoted in the secondary market (i.e. the price relevant to the potential buyer of the fixed-rate note) and the second yield is based on the mid-point between the bid and offer prices quoted in the secondary market.

P is the spread of the yield on a fixed-rate bond outstanding of the given borrower above the yield on an identical maturity US Treasury bond, where the first yield is based on the bid price quoted in the secondary market (i.e. the price relevant to the potential seller of the fixed-rate note) and the second yield is based on the mid-point between the bid and offer prices quoted in the secondary market.

P' is the spread (inclusive of net issuance costs) above the same maturity US Treasury bond yield (based on the mid-point between bid and offer prices) that the borrower would have to pay for fixed-rate funds via a new issue in the bond market.

s is the interest-rate swap rate quoted to the would-be receiver of fixed-rate interest and payer of floating-rate interest, where the swap rate is expressed as the margin above the yield on a US Treasury bond (calculated on the basis of the mid-point between the bid and offer prices quoted in the secondary market) which would be received (with respect to fixed-rate interest receipts) in exchange for the obligation to pay floating-rate interest at LIBOR.

S is the interest-rate swap rate quoted to the would-be payer of fixed-rate interest and receiver of floating-rate interest, where the swap rate is expressed as the margin above the yield on a US Treasury bond (calculated on the basis of the mid-point between the bid and offer prices quoted in the secondary market) which would be paid (with respect to fixed-rate interest payments) in exchange for the receipt of floating-rate interest at LIBOR.

The first lower bound to the margin on a floating-rate note of the given borrower is created by the possibility of one-way arbitrage between the new issue market in floating-rate paper and in fixed-rate paper. Specifically, if

$$m' < s - P' \tag{1}$$

then the borrower in question would find it cheaper to obtain floating-rate funds by issuing fixed-rate paper and entering into an interest-rate swap (as a fixed-rate receiver, floating-rate payer) than by issuing floating-rate paper directly.

The lower bound set in inequality (1) is not absolute. A fall of m' below $s - P'$ will shut off new supply of floating-rate paper by the given borrower. But the margin on existing supply in the secondary market, m, could indeed fall below m' – albeit that the absence of new supply might eventually give rise to a stock shortage reflected in upward pressure on m.

The second lower bound arises from the possibility of one-way arbitrage by investors, in the form of buying synthetic fixed-rate paper, created by an asset swap on floating-rate paper, rather than buying fixed-rate paper directly. Specifically, if

$$s - M > p \qquad\qquad (2)$$

(equivalent to $M < s - p$) then the investor can obtain a higher fixed-rate return by buying floating-rate paper of the given borrower and entering into an interest-rate swap (as a fixed-rate receiver, floating-rate payer) than by buying fixed-rate paper of the same borrower.

Again, the lower bound set by inequality (2) is not absolute. The one-way arbitrage described depends on there being investors wishing to *add* to their holdings of fixed-rate notes issued by the given borrower. Moreover the synthetic fixed-rate paper (created via the asset swap) is unlikely to be as liquid as the 'genuine' fixed-rate notes, in that a disposal would require both a sale of the underlying floating-rate paper and a reversal of the swap position (by entering into a swap deal in the opposite direction). Thus the supply of arbitrage funds with respect to the extra return obtainable on synthetic paper will be far from perfectly elastic.

None the less, arbitrage opportunities associated with inequality (2) can be said usually to *dominate* those associated with inequality (1), in that opportunity of type (2) can exist without that of type (1) being available, but opportunity of type (1) cannot exist without that of type (2) being available.[5] Dominance can be established from, first, recasting inequality (1) in the form (1)':

$$M < (s - p) + (M - m') - (P' - p) \qquad\qquad (1)'$$

and then noting that $(P' - p)$ is likely to exceed $(M - m')$, meaning that, if (1) holds, $M < (s - p)$, which is precisely inequality (2). The likely excess of $(P' - p)$ over $M - m'$ follows from the observation that, first, bid-offer spreads are typically greater in the fixed-rate than in the floating-rate (secondary) market (in line with the greater price volatility of fixed-rate paper) and, second, any premium that the borrower must pay for funds in the new issue market over the rate in the secondary market (where the yield based on bid price is taken as benchmark) will probably be greater in the case of the fixed-rate than in that of the floating-rate market (in that the underwriter is subject to more risk in fixed-rate than in floating-rate issues, on account of greater price volatility and also usually time taken to place the paper with final investors). Even so, when conditions for a fixed-rate issue by the given borrower are exceptionally favourable, relative to those for a floating-rate issue, it is occasionally possible for arbitrage to be profitable in the new issue markets (as associated with inequality (1)), but not in the secondary markets (as associated with inequality (2)).

The third lower bound to the margin on floating-rate notes (of the given borrower) stems from the possibility of two-way arbitrage by the borrower. Specifically, if

$$M < s - P' \tag{3}$$

then the borrower would find it profitable to buy back his outstanding floating-rate notes in the secondary market, whilst simultaneously issuing fixed-rate paper and entering into an interest-rate swap (as a fixed-rate receiver, floating-rate payer).

Note that arbitrage opportunity of type (3) is always dominated by those of types (1) and (2) – only being available when the latter two are both present. But arbitrage of type (3), in contrast to (1) and (2), establishes an *effective* lower bound for m (and M). Any fall of M below $s - P'$ will be quickly reversed by two-way arbitrage on the part of the borrower.

Finally, there is a lower bound set by the possibility of two-way arbitrage by investors. Specifically, if

$$s - M > P \tag{4}$$

(equivalent to $M < s - P$) investors would be able to boost their income by selling fixed-rate paper of the given borrower and replacing it with synthetic fixed-rate paper created from buying floating-rate notes (of the same borrower) and entering into an interest-rate swap (as a fixed-rate receiver, floating-rate payer).

If P' is greater than P – implying that conditions in the new issue fixed-rate market (from the viewpoint of the borrower) are somewhat unfavourable compared to those in the secondary market – then the two-way arbitrage opportunity of type (4) dominates that of type (3). Even in this case, however, the lower bound to the floating-rate note margin set by the possibility of arbitrage of type (3) is more effective than that of type (4). The investor, unlike the borrower, must sacrifice liquidity in exploiting his two-way arbitrage opportunity.

The first theorem – part two

Part two of the first theorem describes the series of upper bounds set to the margin on floating-rate notes by possible arbitrage transactions involving the swap, fixed-rate, and floating-rate note markets (part one dealt with the series of lower bounds).

The first upper bound to the margin on a floating-rate note of the given borrower is established by the possibility of one-way arbitrage between the new issue market in fixed-rate paper and that in floating-rate paper; specifically if

$$S - m' < P' \qquad (5)$$

(equivalent to $m' > S - P'$) then the borrower in question would find it cheaper to obtain fixed-rate funds by issuing floating-rate paper and entering into an interest-rate swap (as a fixed-rate payer, floating-rate receiver) than by issuing fixed-rate paper directly.

The upper bound set in inequality (1) is not absolute. A rise of m' above $S - P'$ will shut off new supply of fixed-rate paper by the given borrower, and eventually (when the borrower seeks new funds) bring an increased supply of floating-rate paper. The latter development would bring downward pressure on m. But there may be a long interim during which the borrower makes no new issue.

The second upper bound arises from the possibility of one-way arbitrage by investors, in the form of buying synthetic floating-rate paper, created by an asset swap on fixed-rate paper, rather than by buying floating-rate paper direct. Specifically, if

$$S - p < M \tag{6}$$

(equivalent to $M > S - p$) then the investor can obtain a higher return by buying fixed-rate paper of the given borrower and entering into an interest-rate swap (as a floating-rate receiver, fixed-rate payer) than by buying floating-rate paper of the same borrower.

Again, the upper bound set by inequality (6) is not absolute. The one-way arbitrage described depends on there being investors wishing to *add* to their holdings of floating-rate notes issued by the given borrower. Moreover the synthetic floating-rate paper (created via the asset swap) is unlikely to be as liquid as the 'genuine' floating-rate notes, in that a disposal would require both a sale of the underlying fixed-rate paper and a reversal of the swap position (by entering into a swap deal in the opposite direction). Thus the supply of arbitrage funds with respect to the extra return obtainable on synthetic floating-rate paper will be far from perfectly elastic.

Arbitrage opportunities associated with inequality (6) are usually dominated by those associated with inequality (5) – asymmetrically to the dominance of arbitrage opportunity of type (1) by type (2) (in part one of the theorem). Dominance can be established from first, recasting inequality (6) in the form (6)':

$$m' > S - P' + (P' - p) - (M - m') \tag{6}'$$

On the same assumption as before that $(P' - p)$ is likely to exceed $(M - m')$, it can be seen that, if inequality (6) holds, $m' > S - P'$, that is, inequality (5) holds. The converse is not true. In sum, if it is profitable to buy synthetic floating-rate paper rather than genuine floating-rate paper of the given borrower, then it is probably already beneficial for the same borrower to obtain fixed-rate funds indirectly from the floating-rate note market (entering simultaneously into an interest-rate swap) rather than directly. The latter arbitrage opportunity, however, can be available for the borrower, without the investor having any opportunity as in (5) to enter profitably into an asset swap to obtain a synthetic floating-rate note. Only when conditions for a fixed-rate issue by the given borrower are exceptionally favourable (relative to conditions in the floating-rate note new issue market) might arbitrage opportunity of form (6) be present without that of type (5).

The third upper bound to the margin on floating-rate notes (of the given borrower) stems from the possibility of two-way arbitrage by the borrower. Specifically, if

$$p > S - m' \qquad (7)$$

(equivalent to $m' > S - p$) then the borrower would find it profitable to buy back his outstanding fixed-rate notes in the secondary market, whilst simultaneously issuing floating-rate paper and entering into an interest-rate swap (as a fixed-rate payer, floating-rate receiver).

Arbitrage opportunity of type (7) is always dominated by that of types (5) and (6). But arbitrage of type (7), in contrast to (5) and (6) establishes an *effective* upper bound for the margin on the floating-rate note, albeit directly in the new issue rather than in the secondary market. Any rise of m' above $S - p$ will be quickly reversed by two-way arbitrage on the part of the borrower (issuing floating-rate paper and buying fixed-rate). The upper limit $(S - p)$ to m' sets indirectly an upper limit to m and M, even if there is some flexibility in the relationship between the two.

The relationship turns on the possibility of arbitrage by investors between the primary and secondary markets. In particular, if m were to exceed m' by an amount greater than the difference between m' and the margin which large investors would obtain on buying part of a new issue of floating-rate paper (by the given borrower), then they could profitably dispose of existing holdings of the borrower's floating-rate notes in the secondary market and replace them by taking up the newly issued notes. This two-way arbitrage involves no risk and no sacrifice of liquidity.

Finally, there is an upper bound set by the possibility of two-way arbitrage by investors. Specifically, if

$$S - p < m \qquad (8)$$

(equivalent to $m > S - p$) investors would be able to boost their income by selling floating-rate paper of the given borrower and replacing it with synthetic floating-rate paper in the form of buying fixed-rate notes (of the same borrower) and entering into an interest-rate swap (as a fixed-rate payer, floating-rate receiver).

If m' is greater than m – implying that conditions in the new issue floating-rate note market (from the viewpoint of the borrower) are somewhat unfavourable compared to those in the secondary market – then the two-way arbitrage opportunity of type (8) dominates that of type (7). Even in this case, however, the upper bound to the floating-rate note margin set by the possibility of arbitrage of type (7) is more effective than that of type (8). The investor, unlike the borrower, must sacrifice liquidity in exploiting his two-way arbitrage opportunity.

Arithmetic of interest arbitrage

The series of lower and upper bounds to the margin on floating rate notes set out in the first theorem, parts one and two, can be demonstrated by the example of a large sovereign borrower, Italy, in summer 1988. Italy made a jumbo issue of $1 billion of four-year fixed rate notes in US dollars, and was reported to have swapped this into floating-rate finance on highly advantageous terms.[6] At the time Italy faced the following illustrative conditions in the floating-rate, fixed-rate, and swap-rate markets:

$m = 30$ $M = 36$ $m' = 17$ (frn market)
$p = 43$ $P = 53$ $P' = 55$ (fixed-rate market)
$s = 75$ $S = 78$ (interest-rate swap market)

Note that the swap rates quoted reflect the readiness of various investment banks to quote a keener spread s (the spread above Treasury yield obtained by the fixed-rate receiver, floating-rate payer) than available in the broker market (where the typical quote s, S, was 73–8) – presumably because they already had would-be fixed-rate payers lined up as a potential counterparty and they were keen to get the Italian business.

The lower bound to m', corresponding to inequality (1), $s - P'$, was 20 points. In practice, market judgement at the time was that a new Italian jumbo floating-rate note could not be sold to large investors at a margin below LIBID (London interbank bid rate) of more than a few points – say, 8 points (8 points below LIBID is equivalent to around 20 points below LIBOR). Taking account of issuing costs, that corresponds to a rate below LIBOR from the viewpoint of the borrower, Italy, of around 17 points – below the lower bound (1) of 20 points. Hence it was profitable for Italy to obtain floating-rate funds by issuing fixed-rate paper and entering into an interest-rate swap, rather than by issuing floating-rate notes.

Such arbitrage opportunity of type (1) is usually dominated by opportunity of type (2). This example provides one of the exceptions. The lower bound set by inequality (2) to M, $s - p$, is equal to 32 points. In practice M was at 36 points, above the lower bound. Hence there was no arbitrage opportunity in the form of investors being able to earn a higher return on synthetic fixed-rate Italian paper (packaged from outstanding Italian floating-rate notes and a swap contract) than on 'genuine' fixed-rate Italian paper bought in the secondary market. The exception to the usual pattern of dominance is explained by the especially unfavourable new issue market conditions for floating-rate paper compared to fixed-rate paper (where conditions are measured by the difference between the effective interest rate the borrower must pay on a new issue compared to the 'bid' yield in the secondary market).

Two-way arbitrage of forms (3) and (4) – corresponding to inequalities (3) and (4) – is in general not profitable unless one-way arbitrage of forms (1) and (2) is profitable. In the example these preconditions are not fulfilled (arbitrage opportunity of type (2) not being available). And the two lower bounds to M set by inequalities (3) and (4) are indeed effective. Lower bound (3), $s - P'$, is equal to 20 points, and is exceeded by M (36 points). Lower bound (4), $s - P$, is equal to 22 points, and is similarly exceeded by M.

Consider next the upper bounds. The upper bound to m', corresponding to inequality (5), $S - P'$, was 23 points. In practice m' was at 17, well below this upper bound, meaning that one-way arbitrage in the form of issuing floating-rate paper and entering into a swap was not a cheaper route to fixed-rate funds than a direct issue of fixed-rate notes. Indeed, the simultaneous existence of arbitrage opportunity of types (1) and (5) is a logical impossibility (m' cannot be both less than $s - P'$ and more than $S - P'$).

The upper bound set by inequality (6) to M, $S - p$, was equal to 35 points. In practice M, at 36 points, was slightly above this upper bound – meaning that arbitrage of type (6) was profitable. The investor could obtain a higher return by buying fixed-rate Italian paper and entering into an interest-rate swap than by buying floating-rate Italian paper. Hence the usual dominance of arbitrage opportunity of type (5) arbitrage opportunity over type (6) does not apply in this case – an exception explained by the especially unfavourable conditions for Italy in the new issue floating-rate note market (relative to those in the new issue fixed-rate market).

Finally, the upper bound to m' and m respectively, set by the possibility of two-way arbitrage, equal to $S - p$ (35 points), is not exceeded. This is consistent with the principle that two-way arbitrage opportunity of types (7) and (8) can be available only if both types (5) and (6) are also present.

For the given relationship of m' to m ($m - m' = 17$), inequality (7) sets an effective upper bound to m of 52 points. (If m were between 35 and 52 points two-way arbitrage of type (8) would be profitable – but the supply of funds to exploit such opportunity is far from perfectly elastic, given the liquidity loss which is incurred.) Inequality (3) sets a lower effective bound for M of 20 points, corresponding to a lower effective bound for m (at the given level of bid–offer spread in the floating-rate note market, $M - m$, of 6 points) of 14 points. In sum, m is constrained within a band of 38 points by the possibility of arbitrage between the floating-rate, fixed-rate, and swap markets. Within that band there are various triggers to arbitrage (corresponding to inequalities (1), (2), (4), (5), (6), and (8)) which limit the probability of m floating into the outer ranges of the band.

Completing interest arbitrage

Let us concentrate on the triggers to one-way arbitrage. Inequalities (1), (2), (5), and (6) can be combined to formulate the following ranges for m' and M respectively, within which one-way arbitrage of the form described is not profitable:

$$s - P' \leqslant m' \leqslant S - P' \tag{A}$$

$$s - p \leqslant M \leqslant S - p \tag{B}$$

Inequality (A) rules out profitable arbitrage between the new issue fixed-rate, the new issue floating-rate, and the swap markets. Inequality (B) rules out profitable arbitrage between the secondary market in fixed-rate paper, the secondary market in floating-rate paper, and the swap markets (all for a given debtor). The hypothetical would-be one-way arbitrager behind inequality (A) is the borrower deciding in which market to make a new issue. The one-way arbitrager behind inequality (B) is the investor deciding whether to make a synthetic or direct purchase.

We can construct two further pairs of inequalities, (C) and (D), which complete the system, in the sense that there are eight inequalities to constrain the eight variables (m, m', M, p, P, P', s, S). The first pair involves one-way arbitrage by the would-be transactor in the interest-rate swap market. Specifically, if

$$M + P' < S \tag{9}$$

(equivalent to $M < S - P'$) it would be cheaper for the would-be fixed-rate payer (and floating-rate receiver) to issue fixed-rate paper and buy back his own floating-rate paper than to enter into a swap contract to this end. Similarly, if

$$m' + p > s \tag{10}$$

(equivalent to $m' > s - p$) it would be cheaper for the would-be fixed-rate receiver (and floating-rate payer) to buy back his own fixed-rate paper and issue floating-rate paper than to enter into a swap transaction. Inequalities (9) and (10) can be combined into the pair (C1) and (C2) which excludes the possibility of profitable arbitrage based in the swap market:

$$M \geqslant S - P' \tag{C1}$$

$$m' \leqslant s - p \tag{C2}$$

It is not possible to make a general statement about one-way arbitrage in the swap market dominating or being dominated by that based in the secondary markets or in the new issue markets. None the less, the likelihood of arbitrage opportunity can be rated. For example, compare (2) and (9). Arbitrage opportunity of type (2) dominates that of type (9) – in the sense that (9) can be available only if arbitrage of type (2) is already profitable – if $S - P' < s - p$. This condition for dominance can be rewritten as $S - s < P' - p$. It is usually the case that the difference between bid and offer rates quoted in the swap market (where these are indicative only) is less than that $(P - p)$ in the secondary bond market (for liquid issues). But actual dealing rates in swaps could sometimes be wider apart, especially if the size of the potential transaction is large. Moreover, P' could be significantly greater than P, where the supply of debt (for the given maturity and debtor) in the secondary market is tight (in the sense that most present holders are small investors who have little intention of liquidating their positions and a large order to buy could bring a jump in the price).

The same considerations apply to the usual dominance of arbitrage opportunity of type (5) over that of type (10). The condition for dominance is again that $S - s < P' - p$. In sum, one-way arbitrage opportunity in the context of the market triangle whose corners are the swap markets, the secondary debt markets, and the new issue markets will more often arise at the new issue corner than at the swap corner.

So far, all the arbitrage opportunities discussed have been triangular – involving essentially the comparison of an indirect two-stage route to a final destination with a direct route in one stage (by one market transaction). The last pair of relationships however, concerns simple 'linear' arbitrage, and is based on the decision of investors whether to buy in the new issue or in the secondary market.

The first relationship, (D1), concerns the margin on floating-rate notes in the secondary market compared to that in the new issue market:

$$M < m' + \alpha \tag{D1}$$

The basis of inequality (D1) is that if the margin below LIBOR (M) available on a purchase in the secondary market were greater than the margin on the acquisition of a potential new issue from the standpoint of a wide range of investors, the new issue would be considerably oversubscribed. The comparison of margins in the two markets differs between investors according to the terms on which they deal in the secondary market (How much commission, if at all? What access to competitive market-making?) and in the new issue market (Are they of the size to obtain a substantial discount from the lead management group in new issues?).

The heterogeneity in arbitrage opportunity means that α is not a predetermined constant and that the supply of arbitrage funds is far short of perfectly elastic. For example a large investor might well be able to obtain a big slice of a new issue at a margin below LIBOR which is barely greater than what the borrower pays (inclusive of issuing costs). The same borrower might have turned the price 'against himself' in executing a large order in the secondary market. By contrast, a medium-size investor, with well developed banking relationships, might be able to deal on highly competitive prices in the secondary market, yet be unable to obtain the keenest terms in the new issue market.

The second relationship, (D2), concerns the spread above US Treasury yields for the fixed-rate paper of a given borrower in the secondary market, and the spread which the same borrower must pay on a new issue:

$$p > P' - \beta \tag{D2}$$

The basis of inequality (D2) is that if the spread (above Treasury yield) on a purchase in the secondary market were less than the spread on the acquisition of a potential new issue from the standpoint of a wide range of investors, the new issue would be oversubscribed. Again, comparison of yields differs between investors, and β is not a constant.

Inequality (D2) completes the system of eight inequalities linking the eight variables, m, m', M, s, S, p, P, P', all based on the possibility of virtually riskless arbitrage (there is some default risk implicit in the swap 'leg' of any arbitrage transaction). There is an additional important set of arbitrage relationships, involving a higher order (but still of low absolute size) of risk, between the floating-rate note and commercial paper markets.

The first relationship stems from the scope for investors to switch between floating-rate notes and commercial paper issued by the same borrower. For example, as an alternative to investing in a five-year floating-rate note issued by Italy, the investor could consider purchasing three or six-month commercial paper issued by Italy, with the intention of rolling it over at maturity into a new issue of Italian commercial paper. Under both strategies the investor in effect holds a floating-rate asset; but, in the second, rate re-fixing involves a transaction in the market place.

There are differing risks and transaction costs associated with the two strategies. The first strategy (the purchase of a floating-rate note) involves higher risk in that the credit rating of Italy might deteriorate during the lifetime of the floating-rate note, yet the relationship of the interest payable to LIBOR is fixed. (By contrast, the interest rate on new issues of Italian commercial paper would rise relative to LIBOR in the event of Italy being downgraded as a borrower.) In addition, the LIBOR yardstick might change in meaning. For example, if the reference banks used in the calculation of LIBOR (and these differ between loan prospectuses) experienced an improvement in their credit status, whilst that of Italy remained unchanged, then the margin below LIBOR on new issues of Italian commercial paper or floating-rate notes would fall, and holders of existing Italian floating-rate notes would correspondingly suffer capital loss.

As against these risks, the investor in the floating-rate note can save on the transaction costs of rolling over commercial paper – a factor of particular importance to the smaller investor. Moreover, he is not exposed to the risk of temporary shortage of Italian paper in the desired form – as would arise if, say, Italy decided not to replace immediately maturing commercial paper with a new issue. (During the interim, the effective margin below LIBOR – based on secondary market prices – of outstanding Italian floating-rate notes would increase.) On the other hand, should he in the future wish to reduce the proportion of his portfolio held in the form of long-run floating-rate assets (whether as floating-rate notes or as commercial paper under a roll-over programme), realization is cheaper in the case of commercial paper (where maturing proceeds are simply not reinvested) than of floating-rate notes (where the cost of disposal in the secondary market is incurred).

The possibility of investor arbitrage, as described, between the commercial paper and floating-rate note markets, can be introduced formally into the demand function for commercial paper D ( ). The function can be specified as D (c, M, γ, δ, ϵ, T, W) where c is the yield on commercial paper (relative to LIBOR), γ is the risk of downgrading of the borrower's credit status, δ is the risk of the reference banks' credit status being upgraded, ϵ represents the probability of a change of strategy (associated with an increased demand for cash). T stands for transaction costs in the commercial paper market relative to in the floating-rate note market, and W is all other factors. D is a market demand function, aggregated across all investors. D is a rising function of $c - M$, γ, δ, and ϵ and a falling function of T.

The supply function in the commercial paper market must take account of the second possible arbitrage relationship with the floating-rate note market, this time stemming from the scope for borrowers to enter into a commercial paper issue programme as an alternative to a floating-rate note issue. The advantages of a floating-rate notes issue from the viewpoint of the borrower include, first, the hedging of exposure to a change in his own credit rating. Second, there may also be transaction cost savings from raising floating-rate finance likely to be required over a term of years via a floating-rate note issue rather than setting up a commercial paper programme with appointed dealers and making frequent issues. Moreover, some borrowers may be uncertain as to whether they will have continuing access to the commercial paper market.

The disadvantages of a floating-rate notes issue compared to financing via commercial paper issues are analogous to some of those relevant to investor arbitrage between the two markets – risk of a change in the credit rating of banks (if their credit rating deteriorates, the borrower could find that the fixed margin below LIBOR set in the floating-rate notes is considerably smaller than warranted by the changed market conditions); and unpredictability of cash needs (a small supplementary issue of floating-rate notes would generally be more expensive than simply expanding the issue of paper under a commercial paper programme).

Thus S ( ), the supply function for commercial paper, can be specified as having the same arguments as D ( ). Unlike D, S is a declining function of $c - M$ and of γ. In market equilibrium, the variables in the given demand and supply functions must be at levels such that supply equals demand. In principle, market equilibrium in the commercial paper market could preclude any new issue activity in the floating-rate note market – as would be the case if δ and ϵ were at high levels.

In practice the effective closure of many new issue markets in overall market equilibrium is an important feature of the bond markets. Typically, new issue markets – particularly in floating-rate notes – are open for only a few borrowers (in the sense that most borrowers would find it cheaper to obtain their desired form of finance by other means). The influences that open and close new issue markets for certain borrowers whilst keeping them permanently closed to others are one subject of the next chapter. Illustrative questions include why the new issue market in top-quality floating-rate notes has been closed for lengthy periods of time (potential issuers finding it cheaper to obtain floating-rate funds indirectly by issuing fixed-rate paper and entering into an interest-rate swap), whilst that for certain lesser-quality borrowers has remained open; and why second-tier borrowers have usually, but not always, found indirect routes to fixed-rate finance cheaper than direct new issues (in the fixed-rate bond market).

The second theorem

So far in this chapter the discussion of various forms of arbitrage has been in the context of one currency only. The possibility of exploiting cross-currency arbitrage lies behind the various inequalities which together form the second theorem. The key central relationship around which the inequalities are built is that the differential between the yield spread on a given borrower's fixed-rate paper in one currency sector of the international bond market (where yield spread means the amount by which the yield exceeds that on similar maturity government paper in the domestic market of the country of issue of the currency), say dollars, and the yield spread for the same borrower's fixed-rate paper of identical maturity in another currency sector (of the international bond market), say Deutschmarks, will tend to equal the swap rate in the interest-rate swap market of the first currency (dollars) less the swap rate in the currency swap market for the first currency against the second (dollars against Deutschmarks). (In turn, the currency swap rate in, say, dollar–marks, will tend to equal the mark interest-rate swap rate plus the LIBOR–LIBOR swap rate for dollar–marks.)

In order to describe the various arbitrage opportunities responsible for the above equilibrium tendency, the following notation is introduced:

$p_\$$ is the same as p in our previous notion (see p. 29) (where it was assumed that the fixed-rate paper in question was denominated in dollars).

$P_\$$ is the same as P in our previous notation.

$P_\$'$ is the same as P' in our previous notation.

p_{DM} is the spread of the yield on a fixed-rate international bond denominated in Deutschmarks (of the same maturity as the dollar bond above) above the yield on an identical maturity German government bond (Bund), where calculation is based on the offer price in the secondary market to the final investor (the same basis as for $p_\$$).

P_{DM} is the same spread as p_{DM}, but where calculation is based on the bid price in the secondary market (the same basis as for p_{DM}).

P_{DM}' is the spread (inclusive of net issuance costs) above the same maturity Bund yield that the borrower would have to pay for fixed-rate funds in Deutschmarks via a new issue in the international bond market (the same basis of calculation as for $P'_\$$).

$s_\$$ is the interest-rate swap rate in dollars, defined in the same way as s in our previous notation, quoted to the would-be receiver of fixed-rate interest and payer of floating-rate interest.

$S_\$$ is the interest-rate swap rate in dollars, defined in the same way as S in our previous notation, quoted to the would-be payer of fixed-rate interest and receiver of floating-rate interest.

$s_{DM-\$}$ is the currency swap rate for Deutschmarks against dollars quoted to the would-be receiver of fixed-rate mark interest together with a final principal sum in marks and payer of floating-rate dollar interest at LIBOR together with a final principal sum in dollars (where the two principal sums are equal when translated at the reference exchange rate at the start of the contract). The swap rate is expressed as the margin above the yield on the reference German government bond (Bund) – where the Bund has the same maturity as the swap and the yield is calculated on the basis of the mid-point between the bid and offer prices quoted in the secondary market – of the fixed-rate mark interest due to be received under the swap contract.

$S_{DM-\$}$ is the currency swap rate for Deutschmarks against dollars quoted to the would-be payer of fixed-rate mark interest together with a final principal sum in marks and receiver of floating-rate dollar interest at LIBOR together with a final principal sum in dollars (where the two principal sums are equal when translated at the reference exchange rate at the start of the contract). The swap rate is expressed as the margin above the yield on the reference German government bond (Bund) – where the Bund has the same maturity as the swap and the yield is calculated on the basis of the mid-point between the bid and offer prices quoted in the secondary market – of the mark interest due to be paid under the swap contract.

$l_{DM-\$}$ is the LIBOR–LIBOR swap rate for Deutschmarks against dollars, expressed as the margin above LIBOR of the interest in marks due to the would-be receiver of floating-rate marks (together with the final principal sum in marks) and payer of floating-rate dollars (at LIBOR) (together with the final principal sum in dollars).

$L_{DM-\$}$ is the LIBOR–LIBOR swap rate for Deutschmarks against dollars, expressed as the margin above LIBOR of the interest in marks due from the would-be payer of floating-rate marks (together with the final principal sum in marks) and the receiver of floating-rate dollars (at LIBOR) (together with the final principal sum in dollars).

The first inequality, (1), rules out arbitrage opportunity in the form of a borrower being able to obtain cheaper fixed-rate Deutschmark funds by issuing a fixed-rate dollar bond, entering into a dollar interest-rate swap (as a receiver of fixed-rate dollars, payer of floating-rate dollars) and simultaneously into a mark–dollar currency swap (as a receiver of floating-rate dollars, payer of fixed-rate marks), than by issuing fixed-rate paper in the Deutschmark sector of the international bond market. Such an opportunity cannot exist if:

$$P'_{DM} \leqslant P'_{\$} - s_{\$} + S_{DM-\$} \tag{1}$$

As an alternative to entering into a mark–dollar currency swap, the would-be arbitrager could conclude, first, a mark–dollar LIBOR–

LIBOR swap (as a receiver of floating-rate dollars, payer of floating-rate marks) and, second, a mark interest-rate swap (as a receiver of floating-rate marks, payer of fixed-rate marks). This elaborated arbitrage opportunity cannot exist if:

$$P'_{DM} \leqslant P'_\$ - s_\$ + L_{DM-\$} + S_{DM} \qquad (1)'$$

In practice $L_{DM-\$}$ will rarely be greater than $0\cdot10$ percentage points.

The arbitrage opportunities described involve a higher order of risk than those behind the first theorem, in that the possibility of default weighs more heavily on the currency swap contract than on the interest-rate swap contract (see p. 4). In consequence, the lower and upper bounds set to variables (in this case an upper bound to P'_{DM}) by the possibility of arbitrage involving the currency swap market are less strong than those set by arbitrage involving simply the interest-rate swap market.

The second inequality, (2), rules out arbitrage opportunity in the form of a borrower being able to obtain cheaper fixed-rate US dollar funds by issuing a fixed-rate mark bond, entering into a mark–dollar currency swap (as a receiver of fixed-rate marks, payer of floating-rate dollars) and simultaneously into a dollar interest-rate swap (as a receiver of floating-rate dollars, payer of fixed-rate dollars), than by issuing a fixed-rate dollar bond. This opportunity cannot exist if

$$P'_\$ \leqslant P'_{DM} - s_{DM-\$} + S_\$ \qquad (2)$$

(equivalent to $P'_{DM} \geqslant P'_\$ - S_\$ + s_{DM-\$}$). The more elaborate arbitrage opportunity, involving a LIBOR–LIBOR swap, cannot exist if

$$P'_\$ \leqslant P'_{DM} - s_{DM} - l_{DM-\$} + S_\$ \qquad (2)'$$

(equivalent to $P'_{DM} \geqslant P'_\$ - S_\$ + l_{DM-\$} + s_{DM}$).

The third inequality, (3), rules out arbitrage opportunity in the form of an investor being able to obtain a higher return on synthetic fixed-rate Deutschmark paper of a given borrower (created by buying fixed-rate dollar paper issued by the same borrower, entering into a dollar interest-rate swap as a fixed-rate payer, floating-rate receiver, and simultaneously into a dollar–mark currency swap as a payer of floating-rate dollars and receiver of fixed-rate Deutschmarks) than on a direct purchase of the same borrower's fixed-rate mark notes in the secondary market. This opportunity cannot exist if

$$p_{DM} \geqslant p_s - S_s + s_{DM-s} \tag{3}$$

The arbitrage opportunity associated with (3) dominates that associated with (2) if $P'_s - p_s < P'_{DM} - p_{DM}$ – or equivalently if new issue conditions in the dollar sector of the international bond market are more favourable (in the sense of the yield payable on new issues not being far above secondary market yields) for the given borrower than in the Deutschmark sector. The more elaborate arbitrage opportunity of type (3), involving a LIBOR–LIBOR swap, cannot exist if

$$p_{DM} \geqslant p_s - S_s + l_{DM-s} + s_{DM} \tag{3}'$$

The fourth inequality, (4), rules out arbitrage opportunity in the form of an investor being able to obtain a higher return on synthetic fixed-rate dollar paper of a given borrower (created by buying fixed-rate mark paper issued by the same borrower, entering into a dollar–mark currency swap as a payer of fixed-rate marks, receiver of floating-rate dollars, and simultaneously into a dollar interest-rate swap as a floating-rate payer, fixed-rate receiver) than on a direct purchase of the same borrower's fixed-rate dollar notes in the secondary market. This opportunity cannot exist if

$$p_s \geqslant p_{DM} - S_{DM-s} + s_s \tag{4}$$

(equivalent to $p_{DM} \leqslant p_s - s_s + S_{DM-s}$).

The arbitrage opportunity associated with (4) dominates that associated with (1) if $P'_s - p_s > P'_{DM} - p_{DM}$ or, equivalently, if new issue conditions in the Deutschmark sector of the international bond market are more favourable for the given borrower than in the dollar sector. Thus if arbitrage opportunity of type (3) dominates that of type (2), opportunity of type (1) dominates that of type (4) – and conversely. Finally, the more elaborate arbitrage opportunity of type (4), involving a LIBOR–LIBOR swap, cannot exist if

$$p_\$ \geq p_{DM} + s_\$ - S_{DM} - L_{DM-\$} \tag{4}'$$

The width between the upper and lower bounds to P'_{DM} (for given values of the other variables) set by inequalities (1) and (2), and to p_{DM} set by (3) and (4), is equal to the combined bid–offer spread in the dollar interest-rate swap market and in the dollar–mark currency swap market, $S_{DM-\$} - s_{DM-\$} + S_\$ - s_\$$. On the basis of typical quotation in the broker market, this combined spread would be over 25 percentage points. In practice the spread could be narrower where the bank with which the borrower or investor is dealing has a 'ready-made' swap counterparty.

P'_{DM} and p_{DM} can stray significantly outside the bounds described above, as these are not totally effective limits. They are built on one-way arbitrage opportunities which by their nature are not always present (a given borrower is not continually a participant in the new issue markets, whilst investors are not continually adding paper issued by the given borrower to their portfolios). Moreover the significant (albeit usually slight) default risk implicit in the currency swap leg of the arbitrage means that P'_{DM} and p_{DM} may have to move substantially outside their bands before large-scale arbitrage transactions occur.

More effective bounds are set to P'_{DM} and p_{DM} by the possibility of two-way arbitrage. For P'_{DM} these bounds are set by the possible arbitrage opportunities of, first, a borrower buying back an outstanding issue of Deutschmark paper in the secondary market, issuing dollar paper, entering into a dollar interest-rate swap (as a fixed-rate receiver, floating-rate payer) and simultaneously into a dollar–mark currency swap (as a receiver of floating-rate dollars, payer of fixed-rate marks); and, second, a borrower buying back an outstanding issue of dollar paper in the secondary market, issuing Deutschmark paper, entering into a dollar–mark currency swap (as a receiver of fixed-rate marks, payer of floating-rate dollars), and simultaneously into a dollar interest-rate swap (as a fixed-rate payer, floating-rate receiver).

For p_{DM} the bounds are set by the possible arbitrage opportunities of, first, an investor selling his holding of Deutschmark bonds (issued by a given borrower), buying fixed-rate dollar bonds (issued by the same borrower and of similar maturity), entering into a dollar interest-rate swap (as a fixed-rate payer, floating-rate receiver), and simultaneously into a mark–dollar currency swap (as a payer of floating-rate dollars, receiver of fixed-rate marks); and, second, an investor selling his holding of dollar bonds (issued by a given borrower), buying fixed-rate Deutschmark bonds (issued by the same borrower), entering into a dollar–mark currency swap (as a payer of fixed-rate marks, receiver of floating-rate dollars) and simultaneously into a dollar interest-rate swap (as a payer of floating-rate dollars, receiver of fixed-rate dollars).

The distance between the bounds set by the possibility of two-way arbitrage are some 10 points greater than those set by the possibility of one-way arbitrage – around 35 to 40 points in total. Even these wider bands are not totally effective. Significant default risk is present in two-way as in one-way arbitrage involving the currency swap market, and so the elasticity of supply of arbitrage funds (with respect to moves of P'_{DM} and p_{DM} outside their bands) is far from perfect. Moreover, in the case of two-way arbitrage by investors, there is the added 'drag' of illiquidity, in that, for example, a 'synthetic' mark bond is essentially less liquid than a 'true' mark bond (taking account of the need to unwind two swap transactions in disposing of the synthetic mark bond).

Lower-cost currency arbitrage

Sometimes lower-cost arbitrage opportunity of a somewhat different form is available within the wide bands set to P'_{DM} and p_{DM} by the possibility of one-way arbitrage as described above. The availability of such arbitrage helps to reinforce the tendency of swap rates and bond spreads to move towards the central relationship with one another as described in the second theorem (see p. 44).

The first type of intra-band arbitrage – and the most common – is undertaken by borrowers choosing between various methods of obtaining floating-rate dollar finance. The choice between two methods – whether to borrow floating-rate dollars directly or to borrow them indirectly by issuing fixed-rate dollar paper and entering simultaneously into a dollar interest-rate swap (as a floating-rate payer, fixed-rate receiver) – has already been described (under the first theorem, part one). A third method is to issue fixed-rate Deutschmark paper and enter into a dollar–mark currency swap (as a receiver of fixed-rate marks, payer of floating-rate dollars).

This third method will be chosen in preference to the other two if

$$m'_\$ < s_\$ - P'_\$ < s_{DM-\$} - P'_{DM} \tag{5}$$

or

$$s_\$ - P'_\$ < m'_\$ < s_{DM-\$} - P'_{DM} \tag{5a}$$

In effect, so long as direct borrowing is not the cheapest method of raising floating-rate dollar finance, the non-existence of arbitrage opportunity in the form of a fixed-rate issue in marks together with a mark–dollar currency swap being the cheapest method requires that

$$s_{DM-\$} - P'_{DM} \leqslant s_\$ - P'_\$ \tag{5b}$$

(equivalent to $P'_{DM} \geqslant P'_\$ - s_\$ + s_{DM-\$}$).

By comparing (5b) with (2), we see that arbitrage opportunity of type (5) dominates that of type (2), in the sense that if it is cheaper to obtain fixed-rate dollar finance by issuing first a fixed-rate mark bond rather than directly, then it must be even cheaper to obtain floating-rate dollar finance by issuing a fixed-rate mark bond than by issuing a fixed-rate dollar bond (and swapping).

The second type of intra-band arbitrage is undertaken by borrowers choosing between various methods of obtaining floating-rate mark finance. The principal three methods are, first, borrowing floating-rate marks directly; second, issuing fixed-rate mark paper and swapping into floating-rate marks; and, third, issuing fixed-rate dollar paper and entering simultaneously into a dollar interest-rate swap (as a fixed-rate receiver, floating-rate payer) and dollar–mark LIBOR–LIBOR swap (as a receiver of floating-rate dollars, payer of floating-rate marks). So long as direct borrowing is not the cheapest method, the non-existence of arbitrage opportunity in the form of the third method being cheaper than the second requires that

$$s_\$ - P'_\$ - L_{\text{DM-}\$} \leqslant s_{\text{DM}} - P'_{\text{DM}} \tag{6}$$

(equivalent to $P'_{\text{DM}} \leqslant P'_\$ - s_\$ + L_{\text{DM-}\$} + s_{\text{DM}}$).

By comparing (6) with (1), we can seek to establish whether there is any dominance between the two types of arbitrage opportunity. Type (6) would dominate type (1) if it could be shown that in general $L_{\text{DM-}\$} + s_{\text{DM}} < S_{\text{DM-}\$}$. Such a demonstration is not, however, possible. Scope for one-way arbitrage between the mark–dollar currency swap market on the one hand, and the mark interest-rate swap market and the mark–dollar LIBOR–LIBOR swap markets on the other, should mean that usually $l_{\text{DM-}\$} + s_{\text{DM}} < s_{\text{DM-}\$}$. But given the greater illiquidity of the LIBOR–LIBOR swap market than of the currency swap market in marks against dollars (equivalently, the difference between bid and offer rates will tend to be greater in the former than in the latter), it does not follow that $L_{\text{DM-}\$} + s_{\text{DM}}$ is less than $S_{\text{DM-}\$}$.

The third type of intra-band arbitrage is undertaken by investors choosing between various methods of obtaining a floating-rate dollar asset. The principal relevant three are, first, buying directly in the secondary market a dollar floating-rate note of a given borrower; second, buying fixed-rate dollar paper (of the same borrower) and entering into a dollar interest-rate swap (as a floating-rate receiver, fixed-rate payer); and, third, buying fixed-rate mark paper (of the same borrower) and entering into a dollar–mark currency swap (as a payer of fixed-rate marks, receiver of floating-rate dollars). So long as a direct purchase is not the cheapest method, the non-existence of arbitrage opportunity in the form of the third method being cheaper than the second requires that

$$S_\$ - p_\$ \leqslant S_{\text{DM-}\$} - p_{\text{DM}} \tag{7}$$

(or, equivalently, $p_{\text{DM}} \leqslant p_\$ - S_\$ + S_{\text{DM-}\$}$).

By comparing (7) with (4), we see that arbitrage opportunity of type (7) dominates that of type (4), in the sense that if a higher return can be obtained on a synthetic dollar fixed-rate note created via a dollar–mark currency swap and dollar interest-rate swap than on a 'genuine' dollar fixed-rate note, then there is a still bigger gain from creating a synthetic dollar floating-rate note via a dollar–mark currency swap than via a dollar interest-rate swap.

The fourth and final type of intra-band arbitrage is undertaken by investors choosing between various methods of obtaining a floating-rate mark asset. The principal relevant three methods are, first, buying directly in the secondary market a mark floating-rate note of a given borrower; second, buying fixed-rate mark paper (of the same borrower) and entering into a mark interest-rate swap (as a floating-rate receiver, fixed-rate payer); and third, buying fixed-rate dollar paper (of the same borrower) and entering into both a dollar interest-rate swap (as a floating-rate receiver, fixed-rate payer) and a dollar–mark LIBOR–LIBOR swap (as a payer of floating-rate dollars and receiver of floating-rate marks). So long as a direct purchase is not the cheapest method, the non-existence of arbitrage opportunity in the form of the third method being cheaper than the second requires that

$$S_{DM} - p_{DM} \leqslant S_\$ - p_\$ - l_{DM-\$} \tag{8}$$

(or, equivalently, $p_{DM} > p_\$ + S_{DM} + l_{DM-\$} - S_\$$).

There is no clear dominance between arbitrage opportunity of type (8) and type (3). The latter would dominate the former if $l_{DM-\$} + S_{DM} > s_{DM-\$}$. Efficient arbitrage between the interest-rate swap, currency swap, and LIBOR–LIBOR market should mean that $L_{DM-\$} + S_{DM} > S_{DM-\$}$. But the relative illiquidity of the LIBOR–LIBOR market does not allow the deduction to be made that $l_{DM-\$} + S_{DM}$ is greater than $S_{DM-\$}$.

Illustrative arithmetic

An arithmetic example of the relationships behind the second theorem can be drawn from market data according to a snapshot on 4 January 1989 (see tables 1 and 2 below). The central tendency described by the theorem – that the differential between the Euro-government yield spread in two currencies (one of which is dollars) tends to equal the differential between the currency swap rate (between the two currencies) and the dollar interest-rate swap rate – is apparent. For example, taking mid-points of the various bid–offer spreads, the spreads of five and ten-years' supranational paper above government yields for US dollars were 96 and 89 points respectively higher than for Deutschmarks; the dollar interest swap less the currency swap rate for five and ten

Table 1 Illustrative swap rates, 4 January 1989

(a) Currency swaps (vis-à-vis US $)					
Maturity	DM	£	JY	Sfr	ECU*	Dfl
Five-year	−7/+13	47/67	95/115	90/110	8·30/8·50	0/20
Ten-year	−15/+5	67/87	57/85	95/120	8·40/8·65	10/35

(b) Interest-rate swaps		
Maturity	US$	DM	£
Five-year	58/65	03/09	75/83
Ten-year	66/71	15/18	84/89

*ECU rates are quoted in absolute terms, rather than relative to a government bond yardstick.

Table 2 Illustrative spread between yield on AAA sovereign/supranational Euro-bonds and on domestic government paper, 4 January 1989

Maturity	DM	£	JY	Sfr	ECU*	US$
Five-year	−65/−72	30/38	75/85	50/63	7·60	25/31
Ten-year	−52/−60	37/45	50/62	61/74	7·75	30/36

*The yield on ECU bonds is quoted in absolute terms, rather than relative to a government bond yardstick.

years' maturity was 59 and 63 points respectively. The spreads of five and ten-year supranational paper above government yields for US dollars were −6 points and −8 points respectively higher than for sterling; the dollar interest-rate swap rate less the pound–dollar currency swap rate for five and ten years' maturity was 4 points and −9 points respectively. The spreads of five and ten-year supranational paper above government yields for US dollars were −52 points and −23 points respectively higher than for Japanese yen; the dollar interest-rate swap rate less the yen–dollar currency swap rate for five and ten years' maturity was −43 points and −3 points respectively.

Note that, in the case of the Deutschmark, the differential between interest-rate swap rates (dollars versus marks) was less close than the differential between the dollar interest-rate swap rate and the dollar–mark currency swap rate to the differential between the Euro-government yield spread in dollars versus marks. For example, the Euro-government yield spread differential in favour of five-year dollars, 96 points, was 38 points greater than the differential between five-year dollar and mark interest-rate swap rates (mid-points used), compared to 36 points for the differential between the five-year dollar interest-rate swap rate and the five-year mark–dollar currency swap rate. The less good fit of the simple interest-rate differential is consistent with the LIBOR–LIBOR swap rate in dollar–marks being in favour of the payer of floating-rate marks (rather than of floating-rate dollars) – equivalently with the mid-point of the bid–offer spread in the LIBOR–LIBOR market being negative (according to the alternative formation of the second theorem involving the LIBOR–LIBOR market, the Euro-government yield differential in favour of dollars would tend to equal the dollar interest-rate swap rate less the mark interest-rate swap rate less the mark–dollar LIBOR–LIBOR rate). An indicative five-year dollar–mark LIBOR–LIBOR swap rate was $0 \cdot 06/-0 \cdot 12$ (meaning that the would-be payer of floating-rate marks is charged a margin one-sixteenth above LIBOR in exchange for receiving floating-rate dollars at LIBOR, whilst the would-be receiver of floating-rate marks obtains interest at a rate below LIBOR in exchange for paying interest on floating-rate dollars at LIBOR).

The deviation of the differential between the Euro-government yield spread in dollars and marks from parity – whether this latter is expressed in terms of the dollar interest-rate swap rate less the mark–dollar currency swap rate or of the dollar interest-rate swap rate less the mark interest-rate swap rate less the mark–dollar LIBOR–LIBOR swap rate – was none the less significant. Were any arbitrage opportunities available? For example, consider a prime borrower seeking five-year fixed-rate dollar funds. As an alternative to issuing fixed-rate dollar paper at an all-in cost of say 33 points over US Treasury yields he could issue five-year mark paper at say 60 points below five-year Bund yields, swap into floating-rate dollars at a margin of 43 points below LIBOR (60 points less the mark–dollar currency swap rate of 13), and then swap into fixed-rate dollars to achieve 22 points above US Treasury yields (43 points less the dollar interest-rate swap rate of 65 points). A cost saving could thus be achieved via the indirect route, albeit that in the process some default risk would be incurred (particularly in the currency swap transaction).

Similarly, consider the investor in Euro-Deutschmark bonds. As an alternative to a direct purchase of five-year Euro-Deutschmark paper in the secondary market, on which a yield of 72 points below the yield on a five-year Bund would be achieved, the investor could purchase five-year Euro-dollar paper obtaining a yield 25 points above that on US Treasuries, swap into floating-rate dollars to obtain 40 points below LIBOR, and then swap into fixed-rate marks, obtaining 47 points below the yield on five-year Bunds. Thus the indirect route to obtaining a fixed-rate Deutschmark investment was attractive, even when account was taken of its associated illiquidity.

Given the existence of these one-way arbitrage opportunities, there were probably even greater 'intra-band' opportunities for would-be borrowers of floating-rate dollars (so long as an issue of floating-rate dollar notes was not the cheapest method of raising floating-rate dollar finance). Obtaining five-year floating rate dollars via a fixed-rate issue of dollars and entering into an interest-rate swap would cost 25 points below LIBOR. Alternatively, issuing five-year Euro-Deutschmark paper and swapping into floating-rate dollars would cost 47 points below LIBOR – a saving of 22 points compared to the previous method (and 11 points for one-way arbitrage by the would-be fixed-rate borrower of dollars).

There could be a similar opportunity for the would-be investor in Deutschmark floating-rate paper – so long as a direct purchase was not the highest-yielding option. For example, a purchase of five-year Euro-dollar fixed-rate paper swapped into floating-rate Deutschmarks (via a dollar interest-rate swap and mark–dollar currency swap) would produce a return of 53 points below LIBOR; by contrast a purchase of five-year Euro-mark fixed-rate paper swapped into floating-rate marks (via a mark interest-rate swap) would produce a return of 81 points below LIBOR. In practice no investor would consider either type of synthetic Deutschmark floating-rate paper as attractive relative to simply rolling over Deutschmark deposits or buying mark floating-rate notes (on which sub-LIBOR margins for top-quality paper were around 30 points).

Chapter three

Arbitrage dynamics

The previous chapter established various relationships between swap rates and yield spreads (both within one currency sector and between currencies) which hold in market equilibrium (defined by the absence of arbitrage opportunity). The present chapter is concerned with how a position of equilibrium is reached from an initial position of disequilibrium, how the equilibrium set of bond yield spreads and swap rates might change through time under the influence of change in the economic environment, and how in the process new issue markets for certain types of securities (for example, floating-rate notes or Euro-bonds in a given currency) might become alternatively closed and open.

The US dollar swap rate

The dollar interest-rate swap market occupies a key position in almost all the arbitrage relationships described in the previous chapter. A first step, thereby, towards understanding the dynamics of arbitrage is to understand fluctuations in the dollar swap rate.

Historically the dollar interest-rate swap rate (for benchmark maturities of five and ten years) has varied within a band set by the yield spread on A and AA-rated US corporate bonds (the lower band is the spread of the yield on AA corporate bonds over the yield on identical maturity US Treasury bonds; the upper band is the similarly defined spread of the yield on A-rated corporate bonds.)[1] In principle, when the swap rate is near the lower edge of its band (that is, at around the AA yield level), many A-rated corporations should find it cheaper to obtain fixed-rate finance indirectly (via first borrowing for say, five years on a floating-rate basis and then entering into an interest-rate swap as a fixed-rate payer, floating-rate receiver) rather than directly. Illustratively, the A-rated corporation might hope to secure bank finance at say 10 to 15 basis points over LIBOR, meaning that it could swap into fixed-rate finance at just below the yield on A-rated paper (in that the yield spread between A and AA paper is typically 20 points or more). When, by contrast, the swap rate is at the upper end of its band, the A-rated corporation would often be able to borrow fixed-rate funds more cheaply in the public debt market than via a swap transaction.

Let us consider some of the influences on where the swap rate lies in the band, and on where the band lies in relationship to US Treasury yields. First, take the side of demand (would-be fixed-rate payers). An important transactor here is the US savings and loan associations, hedging the mismatch between their floating-rate deposit base and their portfolio of fixed-rate mortgages. When mortgage business is growing fast – as during a housing boom – the operations of the savings and loan associations could well put upward pressure on the swap rate (measured relative to the US treasury yield).

Borrowers of credit rating lower than A, and sometimes those of A, generally find it cheaper to use the swap market than direct debt issues towards obtaining fixed-rate funds, and if as a group they have a distinct demand for credit from that in the economy as a whole they can influence the swap rate. One possibility is that the smaller, less creditworthy borrowers take fright more than larger borrowers at a raised possibility of much higher interest rates (as when the economy begins to show signs of overheating), perhaps because they are highly levered and face a higher risk of bankruptcy, and their hedging operations at such times would drive the swap rate upwards.

On occasions in recent years the market for corporate debt, even of AAA or AA rating, has experienced a crisis of confidence. These have erupted when there has been sudden downgrading of well known names – whether Texaco as a result of a legal judgement imposing huge financial penalties or corporations which have been the victims of levered buy-outs. During the crisis, the yield on corporate debt (of all credit ratings) in the secondary market has jumped upwards relative to that on US Treasuries, while the new issue market for such debt has been virtually closed. Swap

rates have not risen in step with corporate bond yields during crisis
– reflecting the lower risk of the corporation as a swap counterparty than as an outright debtor – and so they have fallen to the
bottom of the A–AA band or even below. None the less, the swap
rate does rise in the crisis, under the influence of corporations
preferring to obtain fixed-rate finance via the swap route rather
than locking in the high default premium on fixed rates in the
public market.

As a historical tendency, the yield spread on AA and A corporate debt (relative to US Treasuries) has been at its highest
during the recession phase of the business cycle and at its lowest
during the boom phase – reflecting a cyclical swing in perceived
creditworthiness (which follows a similar swing in profitability).
Hence the A–AA band spread within which the swap rate tends to
fluctuate moves anti-cyclically. From the side of demand it is
difficult to make a strong case that the swap rate will tend to move
either pro- or anti-cyclically with respect to its band. In favour of
a pro-cyclical intra-band movement is the argument that small
corporations might take fright in an overheating economy and rush
to fix their cost of borrowing, whilst in the recession they would
be ready to have a large floating-rate exposure. On the other hand,
demand from the savings and loan associations is likely to be
strong in the early recovery phase of the business cycle and weak
during the last stages of the boom.

Forces from the supply side of the dollar interest-rate swap
market probably tend to drive the swap rate in a pro-cyclical
motion relative to its A–AA band (which itself moves anti-
cyclically). In the recession phase of the cycle, floating-rate notes
are likely to lose popularity as inflation risks subside, meaning that
yields on them would rise relative to LIBOR. AAA–rated
borrowers (whose cost of debt finance above Treasuries would
most likely be unchanged) would see even greater profit opportunity in raising floating-rate finance indirectly (via a fixed-rate
issue and entering into a dollar interest-rate swap as a fixed-rate
receiver, floating-rate payer) rather than directly (either an issue of
floating-rate notes or of commercial paper). There may also be
enlarged profit opportunity for investors in buying synthetic fixed-
rate paper (created by combining a purchase of floating-rate notes
and entering into a swap as a floating-rate payer, fixed-rate
receiver).

In the boom phase of the cycle, floating-rate notes are likely to be at their most popular (as inflation risks increase and the yield curve becomes inverse) and yields on them exceptionally low relative to LIBOR. Thus prime borrowers could find it profitable to tap the floating-rate note market directly, meaning a shrunken supply of interest-rate swaps. Supply would increase, however, if a liquidity crisis erupted under the pressure from the monetary squeeze which accompanies the peak of the boom. In such a crisis – for example, the weeks following Mexico's default in summer 1982 or following the crash of 1987[2] – the yields on A and AA bonds rise relative to those on AAA bonds (particularly jumbo issues), with the latter themselves probably rising relative to US Treasury yields (in that US Treasury bonds are the most liquid of all). The swap rate, in moving up in step with its A–AA band, would increase relative to AAA, especially AAA jumbo, yields, meaning that borrowers able to issue these could obtain floating-rate funds (via a swap) at highly attractive rates. Hence forces from the supply side would restrain the rise in swap rates during a crisis.

Floating-rate note dynamics

The question has been begged so far as to why the US dollar interest-rate swap rate tends to move in the A–AA band, thereby meaning that borrowers of lower credit rating than A will generally find the swap route to fixed-rate finance cheapest, whilst those of AA credit rating or better will generally find a public debt issue the cheapest alternative. (An intermediate zone of A and A+ borrowers are the main 'floating' clients – sometimes finding it cheaper to use the swap route, sometimes a straight debt issue.)

The answer involves understanding the comparative advantage of various categories of borrowers in the different markets for credit. First, there is the observation that borrowers of less than A rating, who are often in addition little known to the wider investing public, cannot feasibly make a debt issue. Only banks with a well established relationship to the borrower are able feasibly to assess the credit risk involved. As bank finance in the USA is virtually entirely in floating-rate form, these borrowers must turn to the swap market when they wish to 'lock in' their interest cost (for short maturities there is the alternative of the interest-rate futures market). Sometimes the bank will act as intermediary for the client in the swap market.

On the other side of the swap market to these lesser-rated debtors are prime-rate borrowers using a fixed-rate issue as a first stepping stone to cheap floating-rate finance (the second step being the entering into an interest-rate swap as a floating-rate payer, fixed-rate receiver). Just as the lesser-rated debtors have a comparative advantage as borrowers from banks, top-rated borrowers have a comparative advantage in obtaining funds direct from the market-place. In most cases the banks are of inferior credit quality to the top-rated borrowers, and they could not justify having a large share of their loan portfolio (beyond what must be held in, say, Treasury bills or Federal Reserve balances for regulatory purposes) earning a lower return than their own cost of borrowing (at the margin). Moreover, even where banks command a top credit status, the prime non-bank borrower could obtain some cost saving by supplying at least a limited amount of paper to investors seeking to obtain a good diversification of debtor risk in their portfolios.

In their market borrowing the top-rated borrowers have a structural advantage in the market for fixed-rate paper over that for floating-rate paper. This stems from the fact that floating-rate paper is in competition (for a place in the investor's portfolio) with short-maturity debt – particularly bank deposits – for which the credit status of the borrower carries less significance than in the market for longer-term debt. (The investor could consider a medium-term strategy of rolling over bank deposits as an alternative to a purchase of floating-rate notes.) Many types of bank deposit are backed by central bank promises to act as lender of last resort. And many investors see advantage in holding most of the floating-rate sector of their portfolio in short-maturity form, as they thereby gain a form of liquidity (frequent inflows of cash – as the deposits or bills mature – at zero incurrence of transaction cost) not available in the fixed-rate sector of their portfolios.

Hence the top-rated borrower will very often find (in view of his comparative advantage in the fixed-rate market) that it is cheaper to obtain floating-rate finance indirectly – via a fixed-rate issue and entering into a swap as a fixed-rate receiver, floating-rate payer – than directly. Contributing towards this situation is demand for swaps from a wide range of borrowers (normally of less than A credit rating) for whom tapping the public fixed-rate debt market would either be unfeasible or expensive (in that the higher is the swap rate relative to the AAA bond yield rate the cheaper is the indirect route, via a swap, to floating-rate finance for the AAA borrower).

None the less, some AAA borrowers will find occasionally that an issue of floating-rate notes is their cheapest route to floating-rate funds. Even in times when inflation risk is low, some important groups of investors, who are not constrained (like banks) to mostly obtaining returns superior to LIBOR, are likely to have some share of their floating-rate portfolio targeted at floating-rate notes. For example, central banks and pension funds might have a much larger share of their portfolio devoted to floating-rate assets than any likely short-run need for cash. They can view floating-rate notes as an attractive component of their 'core' floating-rate portfolio in that there is no roll-over cost at frequent intervals as with short-maturity assets and there are added possibilities for debtor risk diversification (a lower bound is set to the 'acceptable' return on floating-rate notes by the possibility of arbitrage with the commercial paper market). Savings on roll-over costs are particularly important for the small investor, including the important group of retail investors based in Switzerland and Luxembourg.

At times of heightened inflation risk, investors are likely to raise the target share of their portfolio devoted to floating-rate assets – and this additional share would form part of their 'core' holdings rather than those which are to be held as cash reserves. Hence their demand for floating-rate notes could rise strongly. Prime borrowers would find that a raised share of their floating-rate fund requirements could be most cheaply obtained in the floating-rate market (rather than via the indirect route of a fixed-rate issue plus a swap). In consequence the supply of would-be fixed-rate receivers in the swap market would drop. Correspondingly the swap rate could break above the normal upper band of its A–AA range, meaning that even borrowers of just less than A status might find that a direct issue of fixed-rate paper would be cheaper than the swap route to fixed-rate finance. The normal confinement of the swap rate to the A–AA band is a function of the 'normal' degree of comparative advantage which top-rated borrowers have in the fixed-rate (as against floating-rate) public debt markets, and the 'normal' degree of comparative disadvantage which a wide range of 'inferior' borrowers have in the public debt markets compared to in the market for bank finance.

The history of the swap market and floating-rate note market is too short to provide substantial evidence against which to test the hypothesis about how comparative advantage might change under the influence of inflation. During the inflation storm of the late 1970s and early 1980s, when the floating-rate note market thrived, the swap market was in its infancy. Hence the many top borrowers at that time in the floating-rate note market did not have the feasible option of issuing fixed-rate paper and swapping into floating-rate.

The subsiding of inflation risk through the mid-1980s occurred simultaneously with the take-off of the swap market. Hence the new issue market in floating-rate notes was hit both from the side of demand (a receding of the target share for floating-rate assets in investors' portfolios and competition from the new Euro-commercial paper market) and from the side of supply (new opportunities for arbitrage by prime borrowers – in the form of making fixed-rate issues and entering into a swap as the route to floating-rate finance; the opportunities were expanded by the existence of pent-up demand in the new swap market from borrowers previously unable to obtain fixed-rate finance taking advantage of the swap innovation to lock in their interest cost). In addition, investor confidence in the liquidity of even prime-related short-dated floating-rate notes was temporarily shaken by the crisis in the perpetual floating-rate note market (early 1987).[3]

Indeed, in the years 1987–8 there were virtually no new issues of prime floating-rate notes at all. The scarcity of new paper, together with some rise in anxiety about US inflation risks, brought margins below LIBOR on prime floating-rate notes in the secondary market to record highs of as much as 40 basis points in late summer 1988 (a new issue of a prime jumbo floating-rate note could probably have been launched at a cost to the borrower of 20 to 25 points below LIBOR; news of the issue would have brought an immediate setback in the secondary market prices of floating-rate notes, in that relief of the paper 'famine' would be at hand). What issues did occur were for borrowers in the A–AA range – and this observation applies to non-dollar floating-rate note markets as much as to dollar markets.

Like prime borrowers, the A–AA borrowers have some comparative advantage in the fixed-rate markets over the floating-rate markets, in that in the latter they are in competition with bank deposits. However, their degree of comparative advantage (in the fixed-rate market) might be less than that for the prime borrower, as the floating rate which they can reasonably offer would be at a higher level relative to LIBOR (usually at LIBOR or just above) and might well be sufficiently high to attract considerable demand from banks themselves.

A and AA borrowers have less comparative advantage (if any) than top-rated borrowers in the public debt markets over the market for bank finance. The ones which are best placed to tap the public markets are those whose names are well known, even household names, thereby able to attract retail interest. It is such borrowers that have been predominant in the new issue markets for floating-rate notes in the late 1980s. Some of these borrowers have been in a situation where their name is less well known in the international fixed-rate market than in the floating-rate note market (where banks and domestic institutions familiar with the borrower may be interested investors, provided that the rate offered is above LIBOR).

For example, in the dollar floating-rate market during 1986–8 the main non-bank issuers of paper were Alaska, Alberta, Australia, Ferrari, Indonesia, Ireland, New Zealand, Portugal, the State Bank of New South Wales, the City of Vienna, and Yukong. What these issuers all had in common were names that were less than prime, yet well known, and able to justify paying a rate at LIBOR or above on floating-rate paper.

In floating-rate note markets outside the dollar sector, conditions also became unfavourable for new issues during the mid-1980s. On the demand side (of the floating-rate note market) there was the negative of a fall in inflation risk, whilst on the supply side there was new competition from the swap route to floating-note finance. This new competition was usually less intense than in dollars (given that the development of the dollar swap market and demand there were in general much more substantial than in other interest-rate swap markets); even so, there was the potential arbitrage opportunity open to a prime borrower seeking, say, floating-rate marks, of issuing fixed-rate dollars, swapping into floating rate dollars, and from there into floating-rate marks, as an alternative to issuing mark floating-rate notes.

In the Deutschmark sector there was a small amount of new issue activity in 1987–8 by such borrowers as Dresdner Finance, Commerz bank, Amro Bank and Bank of China – all falling into an A to AA category and offering a return equal to LIBOR or slightly higher. Prime-rated issuers who had tapped the Deutschmark floating-rate note market at its birth in the mid-1980s – for example, Austria, Belgium, the European Community, the European Investment Bank, Sweden – did not return; for them, floating-rate marks could now be obtained more cheaply via arbitrage through fixed-rate dollars.

Even so, if these borrowers do return to the floating-rate note markets it is most likely to be in dollars and marks. These are the number one and number two international investment currencies – and potential demand for prime floating-rate paper (denominated in these currencies) even at significantly sub-LIBOR rates could be sufficiently large to allow a jumbo issue (which promises the most liquidity) to be a success. In pounds the prospects for a successful prime floating-rate note issue are less good. The buoyant activity in the pound floating-rate new issue market during 1987–8, at a time when most other markets were in the doldrums, can be explained by the mortgage boom in the UK economy and by the characteristics of the lending institutions.

The building societies, the largest lender in the UK mortgage market, do not command prime international credit status. Hence the swap route to cheap floating-rate funds has not generally been open (the largest societies have sometimes provided an exception). Yet they are well known to, and well regarded by, UK institutional investors and banks. In the context of the mortgage boom the societies had large funding needs, almost entirely in floating-rate form (mortgage lending in the UK is almost always on a floating-rate basis). Their issues of floating-rate notes were of sufficient size to promise liquidity and at rates slightly above LIBOR could attract a large investor public (corporations, investment institutions, and banks).

A similar formula explains the few successful launches of floating-rate notes in other smaller currency sectors. For example, in French francs the 1986 issue by Remy Finance turned on the familiarity of domestic French investors with the borrower. A similar story lies behind the Tunnel Mont Blanc issue of 1987. The 'jumbo' Portugal issue in French francs (1987) depended on somewhat different considerations. Portugal – outside the group of prime international borrowers loved by Euro-bond investors – could not obtain cheap floating-rate funds by making a fixed-rate issue and swapping the proceeds into floating rate. Yet Portugal's membership of the European Community allows its name to be readily marketed to a substantial body of non-bank investors as well as to banks. These could be combined as one market for a large floating-rate note issue at above LIBOR rates.

Windows of currency opportunity

In itself a major fall in the dollar interest-rate swap rate could breathe new life into the floating-rate new issue market for prime borrowers, both in dollars and in non-dollars. Prime borrowers would no longer find it profitable to use the indirect route via the dollar swap market to floating-rate finance rather than a direct issue of floating-rate notes.

Ceteris paribus changes (changes in one variable, all others initially remaining the same), however, are rarely met with in practice, even though they are a popular expository tool in arbitrage statics. Often it is events in more than one market which disturb a situation of initial equilibrium and set off a dynamic process towards a new market equilibrium. For example, a surge in international demand for prime fixed-rate Euro-dollar paper, stemming perhaps from a wave of optimism about the US dollar, could bring simultaneous downward pressure on both the spread between Euro-dollar bond yields and US Treasury yields and on the US swap rate. The fall in the swap rate would come in anticipation of an increased supply of would-be fixed-rate receivers, in the form of prime borrowers taking advantage of the diminished Euro-government yield spread to obtain cheap floating-rate finance via a swap. The new issue market in floating-rate notes would have been dealt a new blow.

In general, none the less, the US interest-rate swap market has more of an independent existence than any other from the Euro-bond markets. Independence is measured by, first, the capacity of the swap market to absorb arbitrage inflows (or accommodate arbitrage outflows). As illustration, consider the above rise in demand for prime Euro-dollar bonds, reflected in a contraction of the spread of the yield on these over US Treasury bond yields, unaccompanied by any initial disturbance in the swap market. Because the dollar swap market is deep and demand there from would-be fixed-rate payers is elastic (with respect to the differential between the swap rate and the upper or lower bound of its A–AA normal band) – the elasticity is explained by the readiness with which, say, A-rated borrowers switch between public debt issues and bank borrowing (together with a swap) as alternative routes to fixed-rate finance, according to which is cheapest – the increased supply from prime borrowers taking advantage of the arbitrage opportunity to issue fixed-rate Euro-dollar bonds (at a diminished yield spread over Treasuries – and incidentally an increased yield spread *below* A and AA paper) as a first stepping stone to cheap floating-rate finance (the second step being the entering into a dollar interest-rate swap as a fixed-rate receiver, floating-rate payer) does not cause a fall in the swap rate by the full extent of the initial contraction in the yield differential between top-rated Euro-dollar paper and Treasury bonds. Rather the narrowing of this latter differential is in turn limited by the increased supply of Euro-dollar paper (from the arbitragers).

If, by contrast, the increased demand for fixed-rate Euro-dollar paper (relative to US Treasuries) were spread evenly across AAA to A-rated paper (rather than being concentrated on the liquid jumbo issues of AAA borrowers), the capacity of the swap market to absorb new supply from arbitrage would be much less than in the previous case (any capacity would stem from low-rated borrowers – below A status – choosing to lock in the cost of floating-rate finance in response to the fall in the swap rate by entering into a swap as a fixed-rate payer). Correspondingly, along the path to the new market equilibrium, the fall in the yield differential between prime Euro-dollar bonds and US Treasuries, and in the dollar swap rate, would be greater. In practice, swings in international demand between different currency sectors of the Euro-bond market tend to be concentrated on the jumbo AAA-rated issues (analogous to certain benchmark issues in domestic bond markets bearing the brunt of swings in investor opinion).

The second dimension of the swap market's independence of the Euro-bond market is its power as a source of influence over the yield differential between Euro and government bonds. For example, a big increase in demand for dollar interest-rate swaps (by would-be fixed-rate payers) – perhaps on the part of savings and loan institutions hedging a large growth in loan business – would bring significant upward pressure on the yield spread of Euro-dollar bonds over US Treasuries. The two points of greatest pressure would be A-rated bonds (from borrowers switching to direct issues of fixed-rate debt in preference to swaps) and just below prime-rated bonds (as borrowers previously on the border-line of where a fixed-rate issue together with a swap would be a cheaper route to floating-rate finance than the direct one are now definitely across it, and become substantial issuers of fixed-rate paper to exploit the new arbitrage opportunity). In turn, the raised yield spreads at the two pressure points would attract investors from nearby sections of the bond market (where near is defined in terms of closeness of credit rating), causing the upward pressure to be generalized.

Several non-dollar interest-rate swap markets do enjoy a signifi-cant degree of independence from the Euro-bond market – even if it is less than that enjoyed by the dollar interest-rate swap market. Otherwise there would not be the periodic windows of opportunity that open up in some currency sectors of the international bond market. Windows of opportunity open where in a given currency a sudden upturn of demand in the interest-rate (or currency) swap market or in the Euro-bond market (for that currency) induces a flurry of new issues driven by arbitrage opportunity.

For example, at various times international investors – and in particular European retail investors, who have a distinct preference for Euro-paper over domestic bonds (largely on account of tax factors) – are drawn to the speculative opportunity in some of the high-coupon bond markets (Italian lire, Canadian dollars, Spanish pesetas, Australian dollars, British pounds, ECUs, French francs). These bursts in demand make it possible for prime well known borrowers (whose names are easy to market to the speculative retail investor) to issue Euro-bonds (in the currency concerned) at yields which are barely higher than those on government bonds, and even sometimes substantially below. Provided that the currency swap market (or interest-rate swap market in the given currency) has some capacity to absorb arbitrage inflows, there would usually be opportunities for some borrowers to make a Euro-bond issue as a first stage to cheap finance via a swap in another form.

As a more specific example, in early 1988 there was considerable speculative demand from Europe for Euro-sterling bonds – on the view that the UK authorities would soon change their exchange rate policy and allow the pound to float upwards. Coincidentally there was lively demand from UK corporates for swaps (as fixed-rate payers), as many treasurers were concerned at the risk that the economy might overheat later in the year and interest rates rise sharply. Hence prime international borrowers whose names were popular with the largely European retail investor could issue Euro-sterling paper and swap into, say, floating-rate dollars (or other currencies) on cheap terms. (Arbitrage-induced flows ensure that demand for pound interest-rate swaps is fully felt in the pound–dollar currency swap market.)

At times, however, the existence of strong retail demand for Euro-sterling paper has not been a sufficient condition to open the new issue window – instead Euro-sterling yields in the secondary market have fallen far relative to gilt-edged yields. This failure of the window to open has occurred when business in the pound swap markets has been thin and demand weak. Then the increase in potential supply in the sterling swap market from prime international borrowers using a Euro-sterling bond issue towards obtaining cheap finance in another form (whether floating-rate pounds, floating-rate dollars, or perhaps fixed-rate marks) brings a sharp fall in the sterling swap rate – causing arbitrage to be stillborn. The non-existence of an active market in UK corporate debt means that a fall in the swap rate does not trigger arbitrage demand from A-rated corporations switching from the fixed-rate new issue market to the swap market (as occurred in the earlier US example). Elasticity of demand in the sterling swap markets largely depends on the readiness of borrowers to switch from floating to fixed-rate finance in response to a fall in the fixed-rate available via the swap market. The elasticity of demand in the very short run is due to borrowers having already decided on a target amount of fixed-rate funds to be obtained over the medium term proceeding to action when the swap rate appears attractive. At times when there is little interest in obtaining fixed-rate funds, even over the medium term, investor demand in the Euro-sterling bond market may fail to open a window of opportunity in the new issue market.

On rare occasions, strong demand in the interest-rate (or currency) swap market of a particular currency has been sufficient to force open the window of opportunity in the new issue market (for Euro-bonds denominated in that same currency) even without there being a sudden surge of investor demand. The occasions are rare because a crop of new issues would be difficult to sell quickly at yields close to prevailing secondary market yields (unless there are, say, many investors in the domestic bond market of the currency in question ready to switch into the new Euro-paper at a yield differential just slightly above the norm), and investment banks are typically reluctant to hold large amounts of new paper on their books over a long period until it is gradually fully digested by final investors.

Perhaps the ECU new issue market is the best example of one opened occasionally from the side of the swap market rather than from that of an upturn in investor demand. The trigger has usually been a new issue of ECU-denominated bonds (of around five years' maturity) by the Italian government in its domestic market. Because these bonds are subject to Italian withholding tax they have sold at yields substantially higher (over 100 basis points) than yields on top-rated similar-maturity paper in the ECU sector of the Euro-bond market and higher than rates (expressed in absolute terms, rather than relative to a government paper yardstick) in the ECU currency and interest-rate swap markets (by around 30 basis points).

International investors eligible under double-tax treaty to a refund of Italian withholding tax have been able to repackage new issues of Italian ECU bonds into attractive floating-rate notes in other currencies, mainly dollars (the same opportunity does not exist in the secondary market for the Italian ECU bonds, given its illiquidity). The investors buy the Italian ECU bonds (at new issue) and simultaneously enter into an ECU currency swap as a payer of fixed-rate ECUs, receiver of floating-rate dollars. Thus they create a synthetic Italy-backed dollar floating-rate note at a yield (net of transaction costs) some 20 basis points above LIBOR (which compares to a yield on 'authentic' Italy floating-rate notes in the Euro-bond market sometimes as much as 30 basis points *below* LIBOR).

The synthetic and authentic versions of Italian floating-rate notes are not perfect substitutes. Even those investors able to reclaim tax withheld on the synthetic notes (there is no withholding tax on issues of floating-rate notes in the Euro-bond market) are still subject to the risk that the Italian authorities will change the rules on eligibility for a refund. Moreover the synthetic paper is much less liquid than the Euro floating-rate notes; the illiquidity stems, first, from the poor secondary market in Italian ECU bonds, and, second, from the need to unwind the swap position. In addition there is the small element of default risk in the ECU–currency swap contract (part of the synthetic package to consider).

Even so, synthetic dollar floating-rate notes backed by the Italian government at yields significantly above LIBOR have excited considerable interest. Hence new issues of Italian ECU paper have typically brought a reaction in the ECU swap market, with rates there rising substantially in anticipation of demand (by would-be fixed-rate payers of ECU) from investors creating new synthetic Italy floating-rate notes.

In turn the jump in ECU swap rates opens up an arbitrage opportunity for potential issuers in the international ECU bond market. The opportunity takes the form of being able to use an issue of ECU paper as a first step towards cheap finance via a swap in another currency. For example, there is the prospect of dollar floating-rate finance at a rate well below LIBOR from issuing fixed-rate ECU paper and entering into a swap transaction (as a payer of floating-rate dollars and receiver of fixed-rate ECUs).

Key to the swap market sometimes being able to open the window to the new issue market in the ECU example are, first, the illiquidity of the secondary market in Italian domestic ECU bonds (meaning that investor demand, particularly from arbitragers, is concentrated on the new issue market) and, second, the fact that the swap rate is below the relevant government yield (in the example, the ECU swap rate is below the yield on Italian domestic ECU bonds), meaning that synthetic government-backed floating-rate notes can be created at yields above LIBOR.

In most currencies, swap rates (expressed in terms of an absolute level, as in the Italian example, rather than as a spread above government yields) are higher than government yields, reflecting demand from a wide range of domestic borrowers (not well enough known to tap the international capital markets) for whom alternative routes to fixed-rate finance (for example, an issue in the domestic corporate debt market, if this exists, or the entering into lease contracts) would be at a cost substantially higher than the government's cost of borrowing. In the case of the ECU, however, swap rates have been such that even less well known borrowers (of

A rating or less) have been able to obtain fixed-rate ECUs (by either borrowing floating-rate ECUs and entering into an ECU interest-rate swap as a fixed-rate payer, floating-rate receiver, or borrowing floating-rate dollars and entering into an ECU currency swap as a payer of fixed-rate ECUs, receiver of floating-rate dollars) at a yield significantly below that which the AAA-rated Republic of Italy must offer in its domestic market.

Factors responsible for that cost saving being available include, first, the popularity of international ECU paper with investors even at yields substantially below their theoretical yardstick (calculated from the yields on the component currencies of the ECU basket). The popularity has been based, for example, on the liquidity advantage of the ECU over many of its smaller components. Second, there has been the unfamiliarity of many international investors with the Italian domestic market in ECUs and a wide range of views about its tax risks and degree of illiquidity. Hence the yield on domestic Italian ECU bonds has remained far above ECU rates in the international market.

Structural elements in currency spreads

The analysis of forces which are capable of opening up the currency window of opportunity is essentially short-run. A subject for long-run analysis is what sustains the substantial differences between the spread of Euro-bond yields over government bond yields in the various currency sectors. In line with these spread differences are differences between swap rates by currency (consistent with the second theorem). Are there structural differences in the supply of and demand for Euro-bonds by currency sector which create an arbitrage potential sufficient to dominate the equilibrium relationship between swap rates (by currency)? Or are there structural differences between swap markets large enough to have substantial impact on the equilibrium relationship between the spread of Euro over government yields in various currencies? Or is there a more egalitarian grouping of forces? What developments in the Euro-bond and swap markets could cause a shift in the present 'normal' differences between currency sectors in Euro-government bond yield spreads?

A starting point to answering these questions is to look at some of the 'normal' relationships which appeared to hold in the late

1980s. First, the spread of prime Euro-dollar bond yields over US Treasury yields has typically been well above the spread of prime Euro-Deutschmark bond yields over Bund yields (which was substantially negative from when the proposal was announced in autumn 1987 to impose a withholding tax on German domestic bonds, including Bunds, until its rescinding in spring 1989). Second, the spread of prime yields in the foreign Swiss bond market over yields on bonds issued by the Swiss Confederacy has been large – even larger than the Euro-government yield spread in US dollars. Third, the spread of prime yields in the Euro-sterling bond market over gilt-edged yields was barely positive and sometimes even negative in the mid-1980s, but became more positive in 1988–9, albeit less so than in the dollar sector. Fourth, the spread of prime yields in the Euro-French franc market over yields in the French government bond market (OATs) has typically (but not in 1989) been more positive than in sterling, but less so than in US dollars. In some smaller currencies (by importance as international investment vehicles) – for example, Spanish pesetas, Italian liras, Danish kroners – the yield on prime-rated Euro-bonds has typically been at par or below yields on government bonds. Finally, in Japanese yen, the spread of prime Euro-yields above 'benchmark' government bond yields has been highly volatile and on average at least as high if not higher than in the dollar sector.

One important factor in explaining these normal relationships is liquidity. In particular, the US Treasury bond market is the most liquid of all bond markets. The liquidity advantage enjoyed by the US Treasury market over many foreign government bond markets is greater than that of the Euro-dollar bond market over the corresponding currency sectors of the Euro-bond market.

For example, the liquidity advantage of the market in US Treasury bonds over the Bund market is greater than that (if it exists) of, say, jumbo prime-rated Euro-dollar bonds over jumbo prime-rated Euro-Deutschmark bonds. Hence, in the absence of any other factors, we would expect the spread of Euro-dollar above US Treasury yields to be greater than that of Euro-mark above Bund yields. Correspondingly the swap rate in dollars would tend to be higher than in marks – reflecting simply the greater liquidity of the yardstick (US Treasuries) for measuring dollar swap rates against than that of the yardstick for mark swap rates. No structural differences of supply and demand between the swap markets need form part of the explanation.

In fact the differential between the Euro-government yield spread in dollars and in marks is greater than can be explained simply by the liquidity factor. There is also an important tax factor. In general, foreigners can obtain exemption from withholding tax on US Treasury bonds (provided their agent fills in an affidavit establishing their non-residence). By contrast, no general exemption is available in Bunds. Rather, investors whose country of residence has a double tax treaty with the Federal Republic can obtain a credit against tax deducted at source on Bunds against their own tax liabilities or sometimes obtain a tax refund. But the procedures are cumbersome, and anyhow not available to a wide range of international investors, even those willing to sacrifice anonymity. Hence Euro-bonds have a greater tax advantage *vis-à-vis* government bonds in Deutschmarks than in US dollars. In addition, German residents are in general better placed to exploit the tax advantages on Euro-Deutschmark bonds *vis-à-vis* Bunds, given the proximity of Luxembourg and the active role of German banks in marketing Euro-mark bonds to their retail clients, than are US residents to exploit the tax advantages of Euro-dollar bonds *vis-à-vis* US Treasuries. The inflow of domestic flight capital into the Euro-mark bond market contributed powerfully to the depression of yields there relative to those in the Bund market during 1988.

Coincidentally the tax factor favouring a lower Euro-government yield spread in Deutschmarks than in dollars has gone along with structurally weaker demand (by would-be fixed-rate payers) in the Deutschmark than in the US dollar swap markets. Equivalently, even in the absence of the tax factor, the differential between the Euro-government yield spread in dollars and in Deutschmarks would be greater than could be attributed to simply liquidity differences. Arbitrage pressures emanating from the swap market (in the form perhaps of borrowers finding it cheaper to issue fixed-rate Euro-dollar paper and effecting a two-stage swap into fixed-rate marks than to issue fixed-rate mark paper directly) would push the Euro-government yield spread in dollars upwards and in Deutschmarks downwards. (In turn the increased supply of Euro-dollar paper and decreased supply of Euro-mark paper brought about by arbitrage in the form described means that at the margin the value of the tax advantage of Euro-dollar bonds decreases whilst the (negative) value of their liquidity disadvantage increases

– and conversely for Euro-mark bonds – consistent with a widening of the differential Euro-government yield spread.)

The structurally weaker demand in the Deutschmark (than in the US dollar) swap market stems in large part from the considerable fixed-rate deposit base of the German banks (including mortgage banks). Banks have large placement power among their clients for fixed-rate bearer notes (*Schuldscheinen*). That placement power was built up in line with the tendency of German banks to make medium-term loans on a fixed-rate basis; and inflation shock – which undermines confidence in fixed-rate investment – was less serious during the 1970s in the Federal Republic than in most other countries.

In sum, there has not been a large population of alienated borrowers in the Federal Republic as in the USA – unable to obtain fixed-rate finance in the public debt markets or direct from the banks, and so forced into the swap market. The virtual non-existence of a domestic German corporate debt market means that German banks would in any case play a larger role than US banks in the provision of fixed-rate finance. So far German banks have been able to meet demand without relying on the swap markets. A useful addition to the fixed-rate resources of the leading German banks has come from their ability to readily market keenly priced Euro-Deutschmark bonds issued by themselves to their clients. (US banks, their credit rating seriously impaired by the Latin American debt crisis, have usually not been able to tap the Euro-bond market on acceptable terms.) The main users of the Deutschmark swap market, from the side of demand, have been foreign borrowers (in particular, less well known names, unable thereby to obtain keen terms – if any – in the Euro-mark bond market) and domestic borrowers seeking more flexible repayment terms than are available on bank borrowing.

Foreign demand has typically been strong in the Swiss franc swap markets and has contributed to rates being high there despite Swiss banks, like German, having well-developed client bases for their fixed-rate notes. The principal attraction of the Swiss franc to foreign borrowers has been its low interest rates, especially for long maturities. Many borrowers have raised funds in the foreign note and bond markets in Switzerland. Even those able to do that have seen substantial advantage at times in obtaining fixed-rate francs via a swap. For example, Japanese corporations who have been extensive issuers of franc bonds and notes, often with equity options attached, have also been large fixed-rate payers in the franc swap markets, choosing this route for flexibility and sometimes lower cost (when Swiss appetite for Japanese paper is at a temporarily low ebb). French and Austrian state entities and the World Bank are examples of borrowers who have had a considerable preference for low-interest francs, sometimes in excess of their capacity to raise funds in the Swiss capital market at their usual prime rate; rather than sacrifice their prime credit status they have occasionally resorted to the swap route. Then there are a whole range of foreign borrowers for whom an issue in the Swiss bond market is not a feasible option (perhaps because of low credit status, the unfamiliarity of their name with retail investors, or a requirement of flexibility as to repayment); they obtain fixed-rate francs by first borrowing in another currency and simultaneously entering into a franc swap (sometimes a foreign bank acts as intermediary, itself entering into the swap transaction and providing fixed-rate francs to the client).

In itself the strong demand in the franc swap markets would have contributed to a positive spread of the yields in the foreign Swiss bond market over Swiss government yields. The strong demand gives rise to arbitrage opportunity in the form of some foreign borrowers being able to use an issue in the Swiss foreign bond market as a first step (the second being a franc swap in which they would be a fixed-rate receiver) towards cheap finance in their preferred currency. In turn the potential supply of franc foreign notes from such arbitragers puts upward pressure on their yield relative to government yields.

Even in the absence of arbitrage pressure from the swap market, the yield spread between Swiss foreign bonds and government bonds would be high in comparison with that in many other currencies. This follows from the tightness of supply of Swiss government bonds (explained by the surplus in the budget of the Confederacy) together with guidelines whereby Swiss pension funds must allocate a significant share of their portfolios to domestic bonds.[4] These two factors would in themselves more than outweigh the tax factor – Swiss domestic bonds, including government bonds, are subject to a hefty withholding tax, whilst foreign bonds issued in Switzerland are tax-exempt – which in itself would depress the yield differential of Swiss foreign bonds over government bonds. Also the depressed yield on government bonds would be associated with relatively high swap rates (by international comparison), in that the swap rate is expressed as a spread over government yields. Almost no would-be fixed-rate payers in the Swiss swap markets have access to the domestic bond market (where yields are depressed by the institutional constraints mentioned).

If it were not for the shortage of Swiss government paper and the strong demand in the Swiss swap market, the spread of foreign Swiss bond yields over Swiss government yields would probably be only slightly positive or even significantly negative – as is the case for the Euro-government yield differential in some other currencies – for example, Italian liras, Spanish pesetas, and Belgian francs, where withholding tax is a heavy burden on domestic bonds. In the case of the lira and peseta, demand for swaps (by would-be fixed-rate payers) has been weak on account of borrowers' reluctance to 'lock in' high nominal rates which include a substantial premium for the investor against inflation risk. Hence swap rates have had to fall sometimes to negative levels in these currencies before sufficient demand has been generated (in the swap market) to open the window of opportunity in the new issue market in response to a burst of interest among international investors. (The opportunity involves, say, a prime borrower, seeing strong potential investor interest in Italian lira Euro-bonds, finding a route to cheap finance in his preferred form – say, floating-rate dollars – by issuing, first, fixed-rate Euro-bonds in lira and, second, entering into a lira swap as a receiver of fixed-rate liras, payer of floating-rate dollars).

In the case of Belgian francs, potential demand in the swap market could well be greater than for liras and pesetas, given the lower inflation risk in Belgium than in Italy or Spain. But tight limits imposed by the Belgian authorities on the issue of withholding tax-exempt foreign bonds, whether in Brussels or in Luxembourg (the Belgian and Luxembourg francs are tied one-to-one in monetary union), have stood in the way of many borrowers exploiting any apparent arbitrage opportunity involving swap-driven issues of franc bonds. The rationing of issues in the Luxembourg franc market, for example, explains how yields there on fairly illiquid issues can be as much as 150 basis points below yields in the Belgian state loan market, despite the swap rate quoted in the albeit thin market for Belgian francs being positive.

Withholding tax is also a burden on the Japanese domestic government bond market. Yet the spread of yields on prime Euro-yen bonds over those on benchmark Japanese government bonds has been substantially positive – and often exceeding the Euro-government yield spread in US dollars. One factor helping to explain both the wide spread and its volatility has been the practice of the Japanese government bond market to select benchmark issues.[5] These are by far the most actively traded and they command a substantial liquidity premium (reflected in the yields on the benchmark issues being well below those on non-benchmark issues). Moreover the benchmark issues are at the forefront of speculative pressure, and so during a 'bull run' their yields can fall far relative to other yields.

The liquidity premium and sometimes speculative premium on the benchmark issues can explain both a substantial spread of prime Euro-yen yields over benchmark government bond yields and a substantially positive swap rate on yen (where swap rates are measured as a spread over the benchmark yield). Influences responsible for the volatility of the Euro-government yield spread and of the swap rate include the changing international (and domestic) popularity of the yen and the shifting relationship between Japanese banks' prime rate for long-term lending and market rates. At times when the yen is in demand by international investors, and also Japanese investors are experiencing increased risk aversion to placement in foreign currencies, Euro-yen yields may well fall relative to Japanese government yields (not always, however, as there may be simultaneous speculation in the Tokyo bond market on an early cut in interest rates).

At times when the prime long-term lending rate (an administered rate) is high relative to long-term rates in the market (including bond yields) many Japanese domestic borrowers (particularly those for whom a direct issue in the bond market is not a feasible option) find it cheaper to obtain fixed-rate funds by borrowing at short-term rates and entering into an interest-rate or currency swap (as a fixed-rate payer of yen) than by taking up long-term finance (from their bank). Keen demand in the swap market pushes up the swap rate and can open the window of opportunity in the Euro-yen market for swap-driven issues by prime international borrowers (whereby they combine a Euro-yen bond issue with entering into a yen swap as a fixed-rate receiver to obtain cheap finance in another form). In turn the new supply of Euro-yen bonds brings upward pressure on their yield spread over Japanese government bonds. (Effectively the nexus of the Euro-yen and yen swap markets can unleash greater forces of competition against administered non-competitive fixed lending rates than in the days when only a few large corporations could obtain finds at market rates.) By the same token, when prime long-term lending rate lags behind a rise in market long-term rates, Euro-yen new issue and yen swap market activity tends to be subdued, and the differential between Euro-yen yields and Japanese government yields comes under downward pressure.

The powerful role which the swap market can play in the Euro-yen bond market contrasts with its weak role so far in the case of the Euro-French franc bond market. Weakness does not stem from underdevelopment – indeed, the French franc interest-rate swap market is active (the would-be fixed-rate receivers including, for example, the various *caisses* – savings banks – which have an excess of fixed-rate deposits over their commercial needs). Rather the potential influence of swap market conditions has been held in check by the strict rationing of new issues in the Euro-French franc market. Despite the rationing, yields on prime-rated Euro-franc bonds have usually been significantly higher than on government bonds, by a margin sometimes greater than in the dollar sector (where the yield on prime-rate Euro-dollar bonds is compared with that on US Treasuries). French government bonds are free of withholding tax (albeit the foreign bank, to obtain tax exemption for its client, must fill in a certificate of non-residence) and in bearer form, and so that Euro sector offers less tax advantage *vis-à-vis* francs than in most other currencies. Moreover, whilst the French government bond market is one of the most liquid, the liquidity of the Euro-franc market is widely regarded with suspicion (international investment interest being largely concentrated in the French government bond market – and the small amount of interest from the Belgian or Lyons dentist being insufficient to provide a significant volume of trading).

The tax treatment of UK government bonds (gilt-edged securities) is somewhat less favourable than that of French government bonds, in that they are generally not available in bearer form and are subject to a hefty withholding tax. There are a certain number of UK government bond issues on which non-residents are able to claim exemption from withholding tax, but a detailed application to the UK tax office giving full particulars of the purchaser must be made for each new acquisition and the granting of exemption is far from immediate. Hence on tax grounds alone we would expect a lower yield differential in favour of Euro-bonds over government bonds in the case of the pound than in that of the franc.

Traditionally the demand for fixed-rate pound finance by UK borrowers has been weak. High inflation in the 1970s caused a large risk premium to be built into long-term rates, and considerable uncertainty about the long-run rate of inflation implied that the real cost of long-term borrowing was also highly unpredictable. In these circumstances UK borrowers developed a distinct preference for floating-rate finance – the exception being the UK government (even the latter sought to reduce the share of its borrowing in conventional fixed-rate form, resorting instead increasingly to the index-linked market). Some commentators pointed to a widespread 'double-digit' illusion among UK corporate treasurers – meaning that they had decided, whatever the economic environment, not to lock in a fixed-rate cost of borrowing in double digits; evidence of the illusion included the bursts of demand (by would-be fixed-rate payers) in the pound swap markets whenever the fixed rate came down into single digits. Sometimes, as in spring 1986, when the descent of fixed rates was combined with an upturn of international investor interest in the pound, the window of opportunity in the Euro-sterling bond market would be flung open. More generally the normally weak demand in the pound swap market was a factor consistent with the spread of prime Euro-bond yields over government bond yields being less in pounds than in many other currencies.

The fiscal shock of 1987–8, when the UK budget moved from deficit into huge surplus, set off forces having a direct influence on net supply in both the Euro-sterling and the UK government bond market, and disturbed the hitherto normal equilibrium solution for the Euro-government yield spread and the swap rate. In particular a dwindling in the total supply of UK government debt outstanding brought downward pressure on government yields relative to other fixed rates, for example yields on Euro-sterling paper. The resulting increased yield differential in favour of Euro-sterling (over UK government bonds) was consistent with investors putting an increased value at the margin of their portfolio (where a portfolio margin should be interpreted as a dividing line between different types of asset) on the liquidity advantage of UK government bonds over other less liquid types of fixed-rate sterling paper (mainly Euro-sterling) as that margin receded. Large (and thereby potentially liquid) prime-rated Euro-sterling bond issues are the closest substitute investment to UK government bonds, and hence the yield differential in their favour moved up less than the differential in favour of other types of fixed-rate sterling assets (for example, smaller, lesser-rated Euro-sterling bonds, or UK domestic corporate paper).

An increased liquidity premium on UK government bonds would in itself be associated arithmetically with an increase in sterling swap rates, as these are measured as a spread over government bond yields. Coincidentally there was during 1988–9 an upturn in demand for sterling swaps (on the part of would-be fixed-rate payers) as UK borrowers sought to reduce their exposure to the new heightened volatility of short-term interest rates; in addition, some borrowers were simply exploiting the opportunity, created by the sharp inversion in the sterling yield curve which opened up from summer 1988 (long-term rates being 200 to 300 basis points below short – reflecting the view that the monetary squeeze just introduced would bring an eventual sharp slowdown in the UK economy when interest rates would fall far), to cut current interest costs by moving from floating-rate to fixed-rate borrowing. Very few UK borrowers have the credit status and international appeal required to make a Euro-sterling issue, especially the jumbo prime-rated type most likely to be viewed by investors as a near alternative to UK government bonds. UK banks have virtually no fixed-rate deposit base out of which to fund fixed-rate lending. Hence the new interest in fixed-rate borrowing had its main impact on the sterling swap market (where banks themselves were active as fixed-rate payers on their own account in so far as they were hedging an increase in fixed-rate lending – from very low initial levels – to the UK corporate and household sectors).

In principle a new equilibrium could eventually evolve in which the outstanding stock of prime-rated Euro-sterling paper had expanded considerably and where the sterling swap rate had risen by significantly more than the yield differential between prime-rated Euro-sterling bonds and UK government bonds, which itself had widened only by a moderate amount. Key elements fostering that new equilibrium would be, first, a highly elastic demand for large issues of prime-rated Euro-sterling bonds with respect to their yield spread over UK government bonds (equivalently, many investors, particularly the UK investment institutions which are the backbone of demand in the UK government bond market, must see prime-rated Euro-sterling bonds as a close substitute to UK government bonds). Second, the expansion of UK borrower interest in shifting from floating to fixed-rate financing (mainly via the entering into interest-rate swaps) must be sustained.

Consider, by contrast, the eventual equilibrium which would result if these conditions were not fulfilled. A strong aversion among the traditional investors in UK government bonds to shifting towards even prime-rated Euro-sterling bonds would lead to their yield spread over government bonds rising by more than a modest amount under the influence of a shrinking supply of government bonds and a new supply of swap-driven issues (of top-rated Euro-sterling). The scope for international borrowers to identify arbitrage opportunity in the form of issuing Euro-sterling paper as a first stage (the second being a sterling swap) to cheap finance in another form would be less than where an elastic demand for such paper existed.

Even if the traditional investors in 'gilts' were to prove receptive to the opportunities in Euro-sterling, a block to its development could come from the side of supply. The block would have its origin in the swap market, demand there being insufficient to fuel fast growth in swap-driven issues of Euro-sterling paper. For example, as the UK economy slowed down, the yield curve again became positive-sloping, and the volatility of short-term interest rates subsided, demand (on the part of would-be fixed-rate payers) in the sterling swap markets could ebb. More generally the demand for swaps could prove quite inelastic (perhaps there are not many borrowers who would switch from floating to fixed-rate finance in response to a slight fall in the swap rate induced by new supply in the swap market from top-rated issuers of Euro-sterling paper). In this case, Euro-sterling yields would rise only slightly relative to government yields and the climb in sterling swap rates might be barely greater (than that of Euro-sterling yields). There would be little expansion in the Euro-sterling bond market.

The above analysis of how fiscal shock might impact on the

Euro-bond and swap markets is an example of a study into how structural change, whether in the swap market or in the bond market, can change the equilibrium solution for, first, the yield differential between Euro-bonds and government bonds and, second, the swap rate consistent with the 'static' relationships of the previous chapter. Changes in the equilibrium solution can have macro-economic significance in addition to the implications for market participants. Macro-economics is the subject of the next chapter.

Chapter four

International capital flows

Just as the take-off of the forward exchange markets in the early inter-war years and then the take-off of the Euro-markets in the 1970s and '80s had major implications for the flow of capital internationally, so it is with the swap markets. In broad terms we can say that each take-off has successively removed barriers – some natural, some artificial – in the way of borrowers and lenders choosing how to distribute their portfolio between different currencies. The coming down of barriers and the freer flow of capital between countries have in turn triggered important shifts in economic policy – generally in a liberal direction.[1]

Currency substitution

The innovation of the forward exchange market made it cheaper to go simultaneously long on one currency and short on another than when this could be achieved, if at all, only by a combination of borrowing and lending.[2] The hedging and speculative activities which became feasible were powerful new forces on international capital flow. Then the growth of the Euro-currency markets made it possible for investors and borrowers to shift between short-term assets and liabilities in different currencies at a lower cost than previously. For example, a Belgian investor could now shift funds from a Deutschmark deposit to a US dollar deposit with his local Brussels bank, whereas previously he would have had to organize a transfer from a bank in the Federal Republic to one in the USA. Similarly a Belgian corporation could switch from Deutschmark to dollar borrowing by instructing its bank in Brussels to switch the denomination of its Euro-loan at the next six-monthly roll-over date, whereas previously it would have had to repay a loan from a bank in the Federal Republic and arrange a new loan from a bank in the USA.

The innovation of the swap market has facilitated currency switching (or what is sometimes described as 'currency substitution') by borrowers in the fixed-rate credit markets. For example, a borrower with fixed-rate Swiss franc debt outstanding can switch at reduced cost into fixed-rate Deutschmark debt by entering into a currency swap (as a receiver of fixed-rate Swiss francs and payer of fixed-rate marks; normally this swap will be 'manufactured' by the intermediary combining two swaps involving the dollar – fixed-rate francs against floating-rate dollars, and floating-rate dollars against fixed-rate marks). Previously the borrower would have had to incur the costs of buying back (or redeeming) the Swiss franc debt and of issuing new debt in Deutschmarks.

Moreover some borrowers – lacking the eligibility to make issues in the international bond market – now have the option of obtaining fixed-rate finance in a foreign currency (and sometimes even their own currency) for the first time. For example, a medium-size French corporation could decide to borrow fixed-rate marks, on the grounds that the interest cost saving compared to French franc rates more than offset the exchange risk (of Deutschmark appreciation against the French franc). Most likely it would obtain the fixed-rate mark finance by having first a floating-rate dollar credit arranged (probably with its bank in France) and then entering into a dollar–mark currency swap (as a payer of fixed-rate marks, receiver of floating-rate dollars). Alternatively the corporation could arrange a floating-rate mark credit (again with its bank in France) and enter into a mark interest-rate swap (as a fixed-rate payer, floating-rate receiver).

Some market critics would take the view that the swap markets, in facilitating shifts between different currencies by borrowers – and even the smaller borrower just described can move readily from the initially chosen foreign currency to another by executing a reverse swap transaction to the first and then entering a new swap transaction – undermines the influence of long-term considerations on market rates. After all, borrowers deciding which sector of the international bond market to borrow in used to be considered one of the key forms of long-term position-taking in the currency market[3] (the costs of redeeming a bond issue early and refinancing in another currency could be heavy and so there was a premium on getting the long-term view, rather than the short-term view, correct).

However, even though the innovation of swaps has reduced the cost of shifting from fixed-rate finance in one currency to another, it has hardly made this the ideal method of taking short-term views on exchange rate movement (a simple position in the forward exchange market would be a cheaper alternative). The potential rewards are greatest for the borrower who forms the correct long-term view and avoids the still significant costs of entering into swap contracts to reverse the initial denomination of his fixed-rate borrowing. The lowered prospective penalty (in the form of transaction costs incurred in switching from fixed-rate finance in one currency to another) on being forced to change later the long-term view, perhaps by the arrival of new information or by a revised analysis of the economic pressures at work, should make borrowers more willing to venture across currency frontiers on the basis of their starting hypothesis about long-run currency trends.

The risk in backing long-term exchange rate views is least between currencies that are closely related to each other. For example, through the years 1980–8 the Swiss franc was broadly stable within a range of Sfr/DM 0·80–0·85 against the Deutschmark. German borrowers, convinced that stability would continue, could see considerable advantage in raising funds in fixed-rate Swiss francs. There has indeed been steady active demand in the franc swap markets from the Federal Republic, largely in the two-to-five-year area. Before the innovation of swaps, German borrowers could have turned to floating-rate Swiss francs in the Euro-market (in the form of roll-over credits). But the prospective profit would be less certain (given the volatility of short-term interest rates). Thus swaps have increased the potential interest elasticity of capital flows between the Swiss franc and Deutschmark. The same point on elasticity can be made between, say, the Deutschmark and Dutch guilder, or (more recently) the Deutschmark and French franc.

Independent central banks often do not welcome an increase in the interest elasticity of capital flows in and out of their currency, as the scope for their own autonomy (from foreign influences) in the setting of monetary policy is reduced. And in the early 1980s central banks, even of the major currencies, when facing a current of capital flow which threatened to undermine their preferred policy, imposed restrictions on the swap market. For example, at the start of the 1980s, in the immediate aftermath of the Second Oil Shock, the Bundesbank was concerned at the extent to which the Deutschmark, already under strain from a transitory large deficit in the current account of the German balance of payments, was being undermined by foreign borrowing, largely on the part of corporations and governments in neighbouring high-interest countries whose currencies were tied to the Deutschmark within the European Monetary System.[4]

In principle the Bundesbank could have slowed the Deutschmark's growth as a *Schuldnerwährung* (borrower currency) by tightening monetary policy, but this step might have sent the sluggish economy into a full recession. Instead the Bundesbank sought by direct measures (short of introducing exchange restrictions) to brake the outflow of capital. One measure was a request to German banks not to launch swap-driven new issues in the foreign Deutschmark bond market.

The aim of the measure was to cut the circuit of capital outflow having its source of power in the swap market. Borrowers in the neighbouring European countries, and some supranational borrowers (in particular the World Bank), were making growing use of currency swaps to raise fixed-rate finance in Deutschmarks (obtaining funds first in, say, floating-rate dollars, then entering into a mark–dollar currency swap), stimulated to do so, at least in part, by the then unusually high level of US interest rates and bond yields. In turn, the keen demand in the swap market presented an arbitrage opportunity to certain well known international borrowers (especially those which had not yet tapped the German bond market) in the form of being able to obtain cheap floating-rate funds in, say, dollars by making an issue in the Deutschmark foreign bond market and then swapping the proceeds (entering into a mark–dollar currency swap as a receiver of fixed-rate marks and payer of floating-rate dollars). In so far as the new swap-driven supply of foreign Deutschmark bonds was placed with German investors (rather than abroad), an outflow of capital resulted. And indeed, at the time, foreign investor demand for Deutschmark paper was weak.

The blocking of arbitrage meant that supply in the Deutschmark swap markets (of would-be fixed-rate receivers) was sharply curtailed and accordingly swap rates moved much higher. (At a raised level of swap rates new supply could come, for example, from borrowers with fixed-rate Deutschmark debt outstanding deciding to swap into cheap floating-rate dollars, thereby changing their currency exposure; or from borrowers who had earlier entered into a Deutschmark swap as a fixed-rate payer deciding to liquidate their position at a profit – by entering into a Deutschmark swap as a fixed-rate receiver.) Simultaneously, demand from would-be fixed-rate payers of Deutschmarks would be dampened by the higher rates. Thus supply and demand in the swap market would balance without there being any direct impact on the capital account of the German balance of payments.

The short-run effectiveness of the block to arbitrage between the new issue and swap markets stands in sharp contrast to the ineffectiveness of various forms of restriction imposed in earlier periods on arbitrage between the forward exchange markets and the money markets.[5] For example, central banks have frequently sought to protect their currencies from a speculative 'bear raid' in the forward exchange market by ordering domestic banks not to engage in covered interest arbitrage operations designed to profit from the national currency having fallen to a steep forward discount. The prohibited arbitrage would have taken the form of the bank switching funds employed in the domestic money market (say, in French francs) into the Euro-deposit market (say in US dollars), covering the exchange risk by buying French francs forward, and so ending up with a hedged return in French francs greater than the domestic money market rate. The switching of funds out of the domestic money market into the Euro-dollar market would have been an export of capital, which the block on arbitrage was designed to limit.

In practice the block has been widely circumvented. To some extent, banks outside the country (including foreign subsidiaries of domestic banks) have been able to conduct arbitrage operations in the Euro-money market of the currency in question (for example, converting Euro-French francs, rather than domestic French francs, into Euro-dollars; in turn, the resulting increase in Euro-French franc rates relative to domestic rates attracts funds out of the domestic market – the form which capital export takes in this case). In addition, non-banks in the domestic country have been able to conduct the arbitrage operations forbidden to banks –

either switching domestic funds on a covered basis to the Euro-markets, or engaging in various forms of leading and lagging.

Controls on arbitrage between the new issue and swap markets are not in general so easy to avoid. Except in the case of the US dollar, it is rare for international bonds not to have a lead manager (or at least a co-lead) drawn from the country of issue of the currency. And the lead manager would hardly flout openly the rules of his national authority. Unlike in the case of the forward exchange markets, it is not feasible for non-banks to exploit the arbitrager opportunity without the active (rather than passive) co-operation of the banks (in that a non-bank cannot lead-manage a new issue for itself).

Even so, blocks on swap-driven bond issues are a clumsy instrument of policy, ill suited to the new era of competition in international capital markets – and, indeed, since the early 1980s they have not in general been imposed. One aspect of their clumsiness is the difficulty of distinguishing periods when swap-driven arbitrage in a particular currency sector of the international bond market triggers capital exports from those when it triggers capital imports. For example, the initial situation of large foreign demand for swaps could be followed by a sharp upturn in domestic demand. New issues driven by the arbitrage opportunity of supplying swaps to domestic would-be fixed-rate payers are not stimulatory to capital exports; indeed, they can – in so far as they attract foreign investment demand – stimulate capital inflows. (In terms of the balance of payments statistics, the floating-rate borrowing in dollars by the domestic entity – subsequently swapped into fixed-rate borrowing in the domestic currency – is a capital inflow, whilst that part of the new issue by foreign borrowers sold to domestic investors is a capital export.)

The extra volatility introduced into the swap market by the possibility of controls on arbitrage (with the new issue market) is unhelpful to liquidity creation there. And the periodic forced closure of the new issue window to currency arbitrage opportunity narrows the range of debtors in this sector of the international bond market, which in turn undermines potential investment demand.

Zonalization

The bond and money markets in dollars have at least three important advantages over those in other currencies – liquidity, depth, and breadth. Liquidity refers to the ease and cheapness of buying or selling, especially in large amounts. Depth refers to the size of potential demand for the paper of any particular borrower. Breadth is a measure of the range of debtors whose paper is available to investors. During the years of a fairly stable dollar against other major convertible currencies (say 1961–7) these natural advantages stood in the way of substantial international borrowing and lending in non-dollar markets. The big increase in the exchange risk of the dollar as the new era of floating exchange rates dawned encouraged many borrowers and lenders outside the dollar zone (those countries whose currencies are closely tied to the US dollar) to shift to non-dollar markets. They could thereby reduce their exposure to exchange risk, albeit at the cost of some liquidity. In particular, investors and borrowers in the Deutschmark zone (the group of countries in Western Europe whose currencies are closely tied to the Deutschmark – the 'inner' zone consisting of the Netherlands, Belgium, Switzerland, and Austria, and the 'outer' zone of France, Italy, Denmark, and perhaps Britain) could reduce risk by increasing the weight of the Deutschmark and reducing that of the US dollar in their portfolios.

Still, before the innovation of currency swaps, the lack of breadth and depth in the Deutschmark markets severely curtailed the scope for switching away from the dollar. Dollar zone – and in particular US – debtors were rare in the Deutschmark (or Swiss franc) bond market (as these were unwilling to assume the risk of Deutschmark appreciation against the US dollar) and so Deutschmark zone investors who restricted their portfolio to including only Deutschmark-zone currencies could not obtain a good international diversification of credit risk. Hence in search of better credit diversification, they were willing to hold a larger share of their portfolio in dollar bonds than other considerations would justify. Borrowers in the Deutschmark-zone countries often found that the amount of capital they could raise in the foreign Deutschmark or Swiss franc bond market, at their appropriate credit rating, was substantially short of their financing requirement. Rather than borrowing at the higher rates appropriate to lower-status names, they were often ready to assume the exchange risk of making an issue in US dollars.

The development of swap markets improved the trade-off between debtor risk and exchange risk faced by investors (mainly those outside the dollar zone) and even more so the trade-off between cost and exchange risk faced by borrowers. Investors are able to buy a wider range of debtor names in Deutschmarks (and other Deutschmark-zone currencies) as a consequence of the new supply of swap-driven issues by dollar-zone borrowers and of the possibilities for creating synthetic Deutschmark paper out of dollar paper via an asset swap. True, the investors might view the political risk of a Deutschmark bond issued by a US debtor as greater than that of a dollar bond issued by the same debtor (in that the Deutschmark bond is subject to the risk of exchange controls being introduced both by the USA and by the Federal Republic) and thereby would still want to hold some dollar paper towards achieving efficient diversification of credit and political risk (the investor is assumed to be a resident in the Deutschmark zone); but the amount will surely be less than before.

Directly behind the supply of swap-driven issues by dollar-zone borrowers in the Deutschmark and mark-related currencies (created by the innovation of swaps) lies potential demand for these from Deutschmark-zone investors (seeking the opportunity of improving credit risk diversification in Deutschmarks). Supply would be small if there were not active demand in the mark–dollar currency swap market. Demand there could come from would-be mark-zone borrowers who previously raised funds in the dollar bond markets on an unhedged basis, simply to avoid paying above prime rates in the Deutschmark sector of the international bond market, but who are now able to hedge by entering into swap transactions (first, converting fixed-rate into floating-rate dollars, then floating-rate dollars into fixed-rate marks). Another source of demand could be mark-zone borrowers whose name commanded a potential scarcity premium in the dollar bond market but who had so far abstained from collecting it for fear of the associated exchange risk; they could now collect the premium and hedge the risk via a swap transaction.

In practice the development of swap markets has been accompanied by substantial further 'zonalization' (investors and borrowers increasing the share in their portfolio of assets and liabilities denominated in currencies belonging to the same zone as that in which they spend their money). A wide range of non-European borrowers have been attracted by swap opportunities to the European markets, where their bonds have often met keen demand, whilst European borrowers have reduced their exposure to dollar exchange risk.

Some European borrowers – in particular governments and the EC institutions – had built up a large dollar indebtedness in the immediate aftermath of the First and Second Oil Shocks. Governments – for example, those of France, Italy, Spain, Sweden, Denmark, and Belgium – sought to cushion the adjustment of their economies to higher oil prices by raising large amounts of external finance. In principle it would have been a lower-risk strategy (in terms of exchange risk) to obtain finance in the Deutschmark or Swiss franc (Europe's two principal international monies at the time). But the governments could not have raised more than a small proportion of their 'requirements' for external finance in, say, Deutschmarks without surpassing the limit of the German market's capacity to absorb their name at prime rates. Moreover, there were political considerations in some cases against large-scale borrowing in the German market (for example, it was widely believed that the French government did not want to be seen as highly reliant on German finance).

How different would European borrowing strategies have been if well developed swap markets had existed? (At the time of the First Oil Shock swaps had not been 'discovered'; in the immediate aftermath of the Second a fledgling swap market had come into being, but in the case of the Federal Republic, for example, was subject to some restriction.) There would still have been some natural limits to the extent of zonalization. European borrowers would have thought twice about swapping dollar into, say, Deutschmark debt, if the effective rate they would end up paying (in Deutschmarks) were far above German government bond (Bund) yields, and by a margin much larger than that between yields on similar rated Euro-dollar bonds and on US Treasury bonds. In that case the assumption of exchange risk (in borrowing dollars rather than marks) might be well rewarded by savings in interest cost.

Low natural limits to zonalization could have resulted from a tight supply of would-be fixed-rate receivers (relative to would-be fixed-rate payers) in the Deutschmark swap market together with an inelastic demand for foreign Deutschmark bonds. For example, if the European governments seeking to swap dollar debt into Deutschmarks had had to compete with active demand (in the Deutschmark swap market) from many small borrowers both in and outside the Federal Republic exploiting their first-ever opportunity to obtain fixed-rate marks, the Deutschmark swap rates could have come under severe upward pressure.

In principle the shortage of supply in the swap market could have been relieved by top-rated borrowers – particularly those outside Europe making their debut in the Deutschmark bond market now that they could cancel exchange risk via a swap transaction and yet be able to collect a scarcity premium (in terms of an issue yield below that on top-rated European debt) – being tempted to exploit the profit opportunity of following the indirect route of making a Deutschmark fixed-rate issue together with entering into a swap transaction (as a receiver of fixed-rate Deutschmarks) to their chosen form of finance. But the relief from this source would soon have dried up if the new supply of swap-driven foreign Deutschmark bonds faced inelastic demand, meaning that their yield jumped relative to those on Bunds.

Efficiency

The natural limits to zonalization are related to limits on the size of efficiency gain made possible by the innovation of swaps. An extravagant claim is that swaps have made it possible for borrowers to completely divorce the decision as to which market to raise funds in (on the basis of where their debt is 'best received' or most highly rated) from which currency to select as denominator; and that it is possible for investors to construct their optimum portfolio of debtors independently of the decision as to what weight to attach to each currency. Reality is short of the claim.

Just because, for example, Belgium finds at a given time that it can raise funds at closer to an AAA rate in the fixed-rate Euro-dollar bond market than in the foreign Deutschmark bond market does not mean that whatever its ultimate currency choice a Euro-dollar issue is the first stage in the route to the cheapest form of finance. Suppose Belgium wants Deutschmarks. It may be that the swapped-in cost of fixed-rate Deutschmarks (derived from first making a fixed-rate issue in the Euro-dollar market) is greater than the yield which Belgium would have to offer on a new issue of fixed-rate Deutschmark paper – even though this latter were close to AA rather than AAA yields in the foreign Deutschmark market (and this could well be the case, given the wide band – resulting from transaction costs – within which mark bond yields can move relative to dollar bond yields without arbitrage opportunity via the swap market becoming available).

In that case Belgium could not readily justify borrowing in the Euro-dollar market – except on the grounds that to accept AA pricing in the Deutschmark market would have an adverse impact on how investors perceived its credit status in other markets. Even then Belgium would seriously consider whether in the circumstances it should meanwhile assume the exchange risk of leaving its dollar issue unhedged, thereby engaging in the 'open' (uncovered) arbitrage operation of borrowing in dollars on an AAA basis rather than in its preferred currency, Deutschmarks, on the more expensive AA basis.

In reaching its decision Belgium might consider the general relationship of Euro-bond yields to government yields in dollars and marks. For example, Belgium might assess that tax factors were depressing foreign Deutschmark bond yields relative to Bund yields much more than Euro-dollar relative to US Treasury yields. Hence the cost of borrowing at an AAA rate in marks would be significantly less than the expected equivalent mark cost (taking account of the expected depreciation of the dollar against the mark) of borrowing at an AAA rate in dollars. By extension, the expected equivalent cost of AAA fixed-rate finance in dollars could be greater than that of AA fixed-rate finance in marks, making even an unhedged issue of Euro-dollar paper unattractive.

Investors encounter similar difficulties in any attempt to construct their portfolio of debtors independently of their currency choice. For example, a dollar-based investor might perceive that Euro-bonds issued by Finland in Deutschmarks are selling at near the AA yield level, compared to the AAA yield level in dollars. This does not mean that he can unquestionably buy Finland in Deutschmarks, counting on the swap market to preserve the yield gain (over Finland's dollar debt) whilst extinguishing the exchange risk. Swap rates may be such that a synthetic dollar fixed-rate

Finland bond yields no more, even possibly less, than a 'genuine' Finland Euro-dollar bond, whilst suffering from considerable illiquidity.

The Deutschmark-based investor could be interested in buying a wide range of debtors traditionally available in dollars, now available in synthetic form in Deutschmarks, and thereby obtaining an improved diversification of credit risks. But in doing so the investor would be sacrificing considerable liquidity and might end up with a return which was low by comparison with that on similar-rated Deutschmark debt. And even if not low, the investor must assess whether yields generally on foreign Deutschmark bonds are depressed more than those on Euro-dollar bonds by tax factors and whether the yield differential between the two is thereby significantly in the dollar's favour, even when allowance is made for expected depreciation of the US dollar.

Democratization

Even if limited, the scope for further 'zonalization' in currency choice brought by the innovation of swaps does add to the potential efficiency of portfolio construction by borrowers and lenders. Also increasing potential efficiency is the new scope for 'democratization'. Swaps have made it possible for small currencies to develop an international investment and borrowing role, which previously could be played only by the currency 'majors'. For example, the second half of the 1980s has seen the birth of active Euro (or foreign) bond markets in Italian liras, Spanish pesetas, Danish kroners, Australian dollars, and the rapid growth of previously small markets in ECUs, British pounds, Canadian dollars, and French francs.

Before the innovation of swaps only borrowers with a 'natural' interest in the currency (for example, to finance operations in the country of issue of the currency) would consider tapping its sector of the international bond market. Few well known international borrowers had a natural demand for, say, fixed-rate Italian liras, and, where they did, it was generally of insufficient size to justify a new issue which would have any chance of liquidity.

Swaps have made it feasible sometimes for well known borrowers to launch issues of reasonable size in the minor currencies whilst hedging the excess amount over 'natural' requirements (in some cases the excess amount would equal the total size of the issue). The incentive to launch an issue is usually the arbitrage opportunity of swapping into another currency on cheap terms. For example, such borrowers as the World Bank, Eurofima, Sumitomo Bank, and AT&T have been able to issue bonds in the Euro-Italian lira market and swap into floating-rate dollars at rates far below LIBOR (by a margin greater than could be achieved simultaneously via issues in other currencies).

Behind the arbitrage opportunity has lain sporadic demand from international investors for Euro-bonds denominated in Italian liras. The attraction has been the high coupon available, which the less risk-averse investors have seen as sufficient to compensate for the risk of devaluation. Such speculative interest has come principally from retail investors in Europe (from Luxembourg, Switzerland, and Germany) and from Japanese investors (who have tended to favour high-coupon bond markets on account of various institutional regulations to which they are subject). None of these investors would have much interest in domestic Italian bonds (owing to tax complications and illiquidity). Only well known names could hope to tap the retail demand. Also essential has been demand for Italian lira swaps (from would-be payers of fixed-rate liras). This can come from either inside Italy (borrowers seeking to 'lock in' their cost of finance) or outside (borrowers who do business with Italy and thereby have a small 'natural' demand for fixed-rate liras).

A partly similar combination of factors explains the take-off of the ECU bond market. As the fashion for high-coupon bonds spread, the ECU, offering a higher yield than on Deutschmarks, yet apparently of low exchange risk, was well set to attract investors. A problem was that not many well known borrowers (other than the EC institutions who have a policy of deliberately promoting the ECU) had a natural demand for finance in ECUs. Scope for 'synthetic' demand (related to arbitrage opportunities) came from two sources – first, arbitrage involving domestic bond issues in ECUs by the Italian government and, second, small and medium-sized corporations in the high-interest-rate European countries seeking ECU finance.

Arbitrage in Italian ECU bonds has already been described (see chapter 3). In essence, the arbitrage profit stems from the possibility for top-rated borrowers of issuing debt in the international

ECU bond market at yields far below those in the Italian ECU market. The profit (equal to the difference between the two yields, adjusted for risk and illiquidity factors) is divided typically between the asset-swapper who converts the Italian ECU paper into a high-yielding synthetic floating-rate dollar note and the prime borrower who swaps an international ECU bond issue into sub-LIBOR floating-rate dollar finance.

The popularity of fixed-rate ECU finance with small and medium-size corporations in the high-interest countries (Italy, Spain, France) is based on the potential to lock in a fixed cost of borrowing below that available (if at all) in the domestic currency whilst being less subject to exchange risk than in Deutschmarks or Swiss francs. Banks (from which the given corporations borrow) have virtually no source of fixed-rate ECU funds and so they satisfy the corporate demand by entering the swap market in ECUs as fixed-rate payers. In so doing they may create an arbitrage opportunity which triggers synthetic demand for ECU finance in the international bond market on the part of prime-rated borrowers.

Just as the ECU has been popular among investors as a high-coupon low-risk alternative to the Deutschmark, so it is with the Canadian dollar in relation to the US dollar. Indeed, on occasion in recent years the amount of new net funds from Europe and Japan going into the Euro-Canadian dollar market has exceeded that going into the Euro-US dollar bond market. Demand in the Canadian dollar swap market (on the part of would-be fixed-rate payers) has been elastic, meaning that the periodic upturns in international investor demand for Euro-Canadian dollar paper have opened the window of opportunity in the new issue market to a considerable volume of business. The elasticity stems in large part from the readiness of many borrowers to switch – via the swap market – between fixed-rate US dollar and fixed-rate Canadian dollar debt in response to small changes in the differential cost. Thus new supply in the Canadian dollar swap markets (an increase in the number of would-be fixed-rate receivers) from international borrowers making swap-driven issues in the Euro-Canadian dollar bond market would be absorbed by corporations (for example, Canadian subsidiaries of US parents) taking the opportunity of locking in a fixed rate on Canadian dollar liabilities which is lower than usual relative to the fixed rate on US dollars.

The concept of 'democratization' extends beyond the new opportunities for investors to buy Euro-bonds in small currency denomination and for borrowers with some natural demand for fixed-rate finance in those same currencies to satisfy it either via a Euro-bond issue (swapping only a proportion of funds raised) or via entering into a swap as a fixed-rate payer (making payments to the Euro-bond issuer who is a fixed-rate receiver). The role of the Swiss franc as a 'borrower currency' has been extended far beyond the natural limits set by the smallness of the Swiss capital market. Foreign borrowers with a particularly keen appetite for francs have not been as constrained as previously by the difficulty of selling large amounts of their paper to investors in the Swiss bond market.

Austria, France, Belgium, Italy, Sweden, and EC institutions are all examples of borrowers who have been keen on raising Swiss franc finance – drawn by the low interest rate and the only modest exchange rate volatility, at least in the short run, between their own currency and the franc. Before the advent of the swap, these borrowers sometimes found the option of Swiss franc finance blocked by bouts of indigestion for their debt in the Swiss foreign bond market. The swap has enabled such borrowers to continue raising fixed-rate finance in Swiss francs even when there is little appetite for their paper in the Swiss bond market. Instead of making a new issue there they can now obtain fixed-rate francs via the swap market – the counterpart receiver of fixed-rate Swiss francs could well be a prime borrower, whose Swiss franc debt outstanding is in shorter supply or who is particularly liked by Swiss investors, taking advantage of an arbitrage opportunity (in the form of issuing franc paper as the first step to cheap finance via a swap in another currency).

Lowering tax barriers

The power of the swap to promote both zonalization and democratization is exercised through expanding the Euro-bond and foreign bond markets beyond natural limits to their growth. In the same way, the swap can lower tax barriers to efficient portfolio construction by investors and borrowers. The expansion of the international bond market (including both the foreign and the Euro-bond markets) in general reduces the effective burden of withholding taxes, particularly those which are levied at a rate well above the international average.

Typically, withholding tax creates a two-tier market in bonds. First, there is the domestic bond market, subject to tax (and often to registration requirements whereby the ultimate owner of the bond must reveal his identity); second, alongside, there is a tax-free international bond market (in the same currency) where issues are in bearer form. In practice the yield differential between the two tiers (after adjustment for differences in liquidity and default risk) is less than the rate of withholding tax, on account of arbitrage flows. For example, some domestic investors (pension funds and charitable organizations) and foreign investors (governments and central banks) may be entitled to a full refund of withholding tax and so they would concentrate on the higher yielding domestic rather than international bonds (where yield is adjusted for liquidity differences). Some investors (mainly institutional and corporate) subject to tax on interest income in whatever form, and not able or unwilling to evade the liability by exploiting the bearer form and freedom from withholding tax of the Euro-bond, would also have a preference for higher yielding domestic bonds.

Also borrowers arbitrage between the two tiers. The most direct form of arbitrage is by borrowers able to make issues in both the domestic and Euro tiers. For example, AAA-rated US corporations can freely arbitrage between the US domestic market and the Euro-dollar bond market (since 1984 they no longer need a foreign financing subsidiary based in a suitable tax haven, through which to make the Euro-bond issue free of withholding tax). Arbitrage is not feasible, however, for a wide range of borrowers. For example, many A or AA US corporations are not well enough known among international investors to obtain as keen terms in the Euro-market as in the domestic market. And lesser-rated US corporations could not tap either bond market directly.

Outside the dollar sector the scope for direct borrower arbitrage is often even more restricted. For example, bond issues both domestically and internationally by German corporations have been inhibited by a stamp tax; this can be avoided only in the case of issues made by their foreign subsidiaries to finance investment outside the Federal Republic. In the case of the British pound, UK corporations face no regulatory or tax impediment to arbitraging between the domestic and Euro-sterling markets. But in practice the domestic market is very small and there are few UK borrowers eligible (in terms of size, credit rating or familiarity to European retail investors) to launch Euro-sterling bond issues. In several countries (for example, Belgium) the authorities prohibit or strictly ration issues of Euro-bonds in their currency, one aim being to limit the scope for tax arbitrage (domestic investors moving from the domestic market into the Euro-market and thereby evading tax).

Swaps expand the opportunities for borrower arbitrage between the domestic and Euro-tiers – and thereby reduce the premium which investors pay for the tax advantage of Euro-bonds – by facilitating the operation of intermediaries. For example, well known international borrowers with no current requirement for fixed-rate dollars can act as intermediary in the exploitation of a divergence between yields in the Euro-dollar and domestic bond market (the Euro yield being lower for identically rated debtors) by issuing Euro-dollar paper and passing the proceeds on, via a swap, to a US domestic borrower, ineligible himself to tap the Euro-bond market. The reward for acting as intermediary is a share of the arbitrage profits, and this is taken in the form of saving in interest costs on his ultimate financing package (whether this equates to floating-rate dollar borrowing or some other form of finance) achieved by pursuing the indirect route via the swap market and Euro-dollar fixed-rate market rather than a direct route. The rest of the arbitrage profit (net of transaction costs) goes to the domestic US borrower able to reduce the cost of his fixed-rate financing by achieving this via a swap rather than by other means (for example, an issue in the US domestic corporate bond market).

Key to borrower arbitrage by intermediaries is assurance that the fixed-rate income received under the swap contract will not be subject to withholding tax or any other tax penalty. This is usually the case, as tax authorities do not look beneath the surface of net interest paid between the swap counterparties and it does not become subject to withholding tax. Also key is an elastic supply of domestic arbitragers ready to switch between direct fixed-rate borrowing (from the market or the banks) and indirect (via a swap deal) in response to changes in the cost differential between the two. In practice, this elasticity is probably greatest in the USA (given the large domestic bond market there, and the readiness of many borrowers to switch between bond issues and floating-rate finance hedged by a swap transaction).

In the Federal Republic, by contrast, the same elasticity is low, in view of domestic corporate bond issues rarely being a feasible option, and the role of banks in providing fixed-rate finance. Many corporations would be unwilling to jeopardize a long-term banking relationship by turning down an offer of fixed-rate finance because it appeared slightly more expensive than what could be achieved in-directly via a swap (this would involve, anyhow, the arranging of floating-rate finance, which might not be available for as long a term as fixed-rate). Banks themselves could arbitrage between the domes-tic market in their fixed-rate notes and fixed-rate marks via a swap (taking on short-term deposits and entering into swaps as fixed-rate payers). But they might be unwilling to rein back on note issues and thereby possibly lose part of their natural fixed-rate deposit base in the long run for the sake of a short-run cost advantage.

Hence swap arbitrage would be less effective in breaking down any given initial size of tax barrier between the Euro and domestic bond market in Deutschmarks than the same size of barrier in US dollars (the eventual differential size of tax barriers being balanced by a differential between dollar and mark swap rates). The general rule is that the power of swap arbitrage to knock down a tax barrier (between the Euro and domestic market) is enhanced by elasticity of demand in the swap market. Another general rule is that, for any given currency, this power is a declining function of the size of tax barriers in other currencies (and may even go into reverse, raising the barrier for the given currency if barriers elsewhere are far higher).

For example, were the average rate of withholding tax to rise in European domestic bond markets, the differential of domestic over Euro-yields would rise not just for European currencies but also – albeit to a lesser extent – for the US dollar. The initial fall in Euro-bond relative to domestic bond yields in Europe would induce some shift in arbitrage intermediaries away from the dollar markets. Instead of these intermediaries issuing Euro-dollar fixed-rate bonds as the first step to obtaining cheap finance (the second being a dollar swap) some would now see greater profit in making, say, a Euro-mark issue their first step, followed by a mark swap.

In sum, the possibility of indirect arbitrage via swaps by borrowers should lower the average size of tax barrier between the

Euro and domestic bond market across all currencies – meaning that the average yield in the tax-free Euro-tier rises. The difference between the largest and smallest barriers should also tend to decrease. Some initially very low barriers might even increase slightly (as previous issuers in the Euro-bond market of the low-barrier currency now find it cheaper to issue a high-barrier currency and enter into a swap). Where the initial barrier is zero, however, it will remain zero.

This last case is not trivial. It corresponds to the situation of the Deutschmark from the end of 1984 (when a coupon tax on foreign holdings of domestic German bonds was abolished) until autumn 1987 (when plans were announced to introduce a withholding tax on domestic bonds and deposits as from 1 January 1989). The reduction of tax barriers between Euro and domestic bond markets in other currencies during the period when there was no with-holding tax in the Federal Republic was an influence putting upward pressure on Deutschmark yields both in the Euro and in the domestic sector, in that competition (for investors) from Euro-bonds in other currencies increased (in that the effective tax premium on Euro-bonds fell, on average).

How the Deutschmark and other bond markets responded to the announcement of plans to introduce withholding tax (at the rate of ten per cent) provides an interesting case study of the role of swap markets in promoting 'tax arbitrage'. The announcement brought an immediate rise in the Euro-Deutschmark bond market and fall in the Bund market. Whereas, just prior to the announcement, AAA yields in the Euro-Deutschmark bond market were some 20–30 points higher than Bund yields (which were around 6½ per cent) they fell immediately to around 10 to 20 points below Bund yields.

In determining whether that was an excessive reaction the analyst had to look at the various possible channels of tax arbitrage through which funds might flow, including those created via swap transactions. First, there were limited opportunities for German borrowers via foreign subsidiaries to tap the Euro-Deutschmark bond market for financing investment outside the Federal Republic. Second, German banks could issue Euro-mark paper to fund their foreign subsidiaries, which in turn could lend to German domestic borrowers. Third, it might be profitable for prime-rated foreign borrowers to act as intermediaries in arbitrage between the

Euro-mark and domestic German bond markets, issuing fixed-rate mark paper and entering into a mark swap (as a fixed-rate receiver) where the eventual counterpart would be a domestic German borrower; the intermediary's profit would be derived from the indirect route via the Euro-mark bond market and mark swap market to his chosen form of finance being cheaper than the direct route or other possible indirect routes.

There were other possible channels of higher risk tax arbitrage. For example, investors could decide in view of the fall in Euro-mark bond yields relative to Euro-mark deposit rates (the latter remained virtually at par with equivalent domestic deposit rates, as banks can arbitrage freely between the German money market and the Euro-Deutschmark money market) to switch from Euro-mark bonds to Euro-mark deposits. Some borrowers of floating-rate funds in the Euro-mark markets (most likely in the form of roll-over credits from banks with the interest cost fixed with reference to LIBOR) might switch to the Euro-mark bond market. Where the borrower lacked the eligibility to make a bond issue, arbitrage could occur indirectly. A prime international borrower would act as intermediary by issuing fixed-rate paper in the Euro-bond market and passing on some of the advantage of lowered yields there to less prime non-German borrowers switching to fixed-rate finance from floating-rate Euro-mark finance via a swap (the less prime borrower entering the swap as a fixed-rate payer).

Some channels of arbitrage involved an element of foreign exchange risk. For example, investors could be attracted to Dutch government bonds and Euro-Dutch guilder bonds as an alternative to the now more expensive Euro-Deutschmark bonds. The attractions of Dutch bonds stemmed from, first, the virtually fixed exchange rate between the Dutch guilder and the Deutschmark and, second, the fact that Dutch government paper is free of withholding tax and available in bearer form (albeit not fully bearer in the sense of the Euro-bond market, in that anonymous coupon-clipping is not in general feasible). The demand for Dutch bonds could have a counterpart in some investors, able under double tax treaty to obtain full credit against the new German withholding tax, switching from the Dutch to the German government bond market. There could also be some swap-driven increase in the supply of Euro-guilder paper. Dutch swap rates (expressed in absolute terms rather than as a spread over government yields) would move down with Dutch bond yields and decrease relative to German fixed rates and mark swap rates. (The latter, under arbitrage pressure from the Euro-mark bond market might decrease as a spread over Bund yields but probably not in absolute terms, given the rise of the latter in response to the tax shock.) This differential movement in rates could encourage some borrowers (unable to tap the Euro-mark bond market) to switch from fixed-rate marks to fixed-rate guilders via a swap. In turn, the new demand in the guilder swap market might create an arbitrage opportunity for swap-driven issues in the Euro-guilder bond market.

In fact, despite all the possible arbitrage channels described – and there were still others, albeit of higher risk, involving, for example, the French government bond market or the ECU bond market – and the potential of swaps to widen the channels, the yield on Euro-mark bonds fell even further relative to German domestic yields in the year that followed the initial announcement of the withholding tax. At one stage the yield on five-year AAA Euro-mark paper fell to as much as 70 points below Bund yields. What, if anything, went wrong?

Arbitrage in the forms described did certainly occur. There was a boom in the Euro-Deutschmark new issue market – both on the part of German bank and multinational borrowers and on that of prime-rated foreign borrowers exploiting arbitrage opportunities via the swap market. There was an increase in international investor interest in Euro-mark floating-rate assets; Dutch government bonds were in demand. But the amount of arbitrage was insufficient to check the forces making for a further decline of Euro-mark bond yields relative to domestic German bond yields.

One of these forces was capital flight. German investors were concerned that the withholding tax would open the door to the fiscal authorities discovering large amounts of their previously undeclared wealth (held in domestic financial assets). Hence they transferred funds to Luxembourg and into the Euro-bond market, an important destination being the Euro-Deutschmark bond market. In addition, there was speculation that the initial rate set of ten per cent for the new withholding tax would be raised subsequently, perhaps as part of an EC plan to harmonize the taxation of savings.

There were several factors constraining the extent of indirect borrower arbitrage via the swap markets between the Euro-mark bond market and the domestic German bond market. First, it was not until late summer 1988 that detailed legislation on the withholding tax was published. Before then, foreign borrowers issuing Euro-Deutschmark paper and entering into, say, a mark–dollar currency swap (as a fixed-rate receiver of marks) could not be confident that the fixed-rate marks received from the German counterparty would be free of withholding tax (in the final legislation swaps were indeed outside the scope of the tax).[6]

Second, on the eve of the withholding tax plan announcement, yields in the Euro-mark bond market were substantially higher than the theoretical parity level according to the second theorem (chapter 2). According to the theorem, the yield on, say, five-year Euro-Deutschmark paper should tend to equal that on identically rated five-year Euro-dollar paper less the five-year dollar interest-rate swap rate plus the mark–dollar currency swap rate. In fact, Euro-Deutschmark yields were some 30 points above par. Even the Swiss banks had deserted the Euro-mark bond market for the withholding tax-free Bund market. The new issue Deutschmark market had virtually closed down, as any prospective borrower there would have been impressed by the relative cheapness of more indirect routes to fixed-rate Deutschmark finance – issuing in other currency sectors of the international bond market and swapping. Hence Euro-mark bond yields could fall by 40 points or more relative to Bunds without swap-assisted arbitrage between the domestic and Euro-mark bond markets becoming significantly profitable.

Third, there were competing opportunities for swap-driven arbitrage outside the Deutschmark sector. These began to appear after a three-month interruption, following the world equity market crash of October 1987, during which time swap rates and Euro-government yield spreads jumped amidst a panic flight into liquidity. As the view gained ground that the dollar's major downward adjustment was now over, demand from Europe and Japan for Euro-dollar bonds increased sharply, and the spread of their yields over US government yields fell. Prime-rated borrowers could obtain floating-rate funds at enlarged margins below LIBOR by issuing fixed-rate paper in the Euro-dollar market and entering into a swap (as a fixed-rate dollar receiver). Even larger arbitrage opportunities were sometimes available in other currency sectors of the international bond market – for example, Canadian dollars, Australian dollars, and ECUs.

Flow statistics

The large amount of swap-driven arbitrage in the international bond market – of which the above case study on the Deutschmark provides an example – add further to the difficulties in interpreting national balance of payments statistics. Already the take-off of the Euro-bond and Euro-deposit markets had considerably clouded the meaning of national data on capital flows. For example, a large part of what appears in the US capital account as inflows through the banking sector could be merely a reflection of Japanese and European investors buying Euro-dollar bonds issued by borrowers outside the USA who are using the proceeds to repay loans to US banks. It is the Japanese and European demand for dollar bonds that is of interest in appraising the force of capital inflow to the USA, not the passive reactions of US banks.

The impact of swap transactions on capital account statistics can be illustrated with a number of examples. First, consider how UK capital account data would reflect a burst of new issue activity in the Euro-sterling bond market, most of which is driven by arbitrage opportunity involving the swap market – the opportunity having its source in speculative demand from continental Europe. Foreign purchases of Euro-sterling bonds issued by non-UK debtors do not appear directly in the balance of payments statistics. (These record transactions between residents and non-residents, not between non-residents and non-residents.) Rather, the purchases would be reflected in a bulge of short-term capital inflows, in so far as the swap counterparties to the non-UK issuers are UK residents. These would usually be corporations attracted by the opportunity of fixing their interest costs at a keen rate – doing so by, say, borrowing Euro-dollars from a UK bank and entering into a dollar–pound swap as a payer of fixed-rate pounds, receiver of floating-rate dollars. It is the increase in the UK bank's net borrowing from abroad which is captured by the balance of payments statistics. Yet the statistically invisible foreign demand for Euro-sterling bonds is the important economic fact, rather than the bank's foreign borrowing, towards understanding the nature of the capital inflow to the UK.

The second example is drawn from the Swiss franc markets. Suppose in a given year there had been a strong tendency for non-Swiss borrowers to shift out of fixed-rate franc liabilities via entering into swaps (as receivers of fixed-rate francs, payers of floating-rate dollars), perhaps driven by a perception that the probability had increased of a big appreciation of the Swiss franc. The counterparts in these swaps to 'old' foreign borrowers would include 'new' foreign borrowers – who would normally have tapped the Swiss bond foreign bond market but are attracted instead by the cheap rate on swaps – and Swiss domestic borrowers (drawn by the flexibility and reduced cost of synthetic fixed-rate francs, created by borrowing, say, floating-rate dollars and entering into a franc–dollar swap, compared to fixed-rate francs obtained directly). Thus in the Swiss balance of payments the shift out of franc debt by 'old' foreign borrowers – the economically meaningful transaction – would be reflected in, first, diminished purchases of foreign franc bonds by Swiss residents (in line with decreased new issue volume) and a fall in net short-term lending abroad by the banks.

In the example of the introduction of withholding tax in the Federal Republic, the fall-off in foreign demand for German government bonds and the surge in purchases of swap-driven issues by foreign borrowers in the Euro-Deutschmark bond market contributed to an apparent huge deterioration in the long-term capital account of the German balance of payments during 1988 (other contributors included German purchases of Euro-bonds denominated in foreign currencies). But the deterioration over-stated economic reality, as did the apparent improvement in the short-term capital account. A big increase in foreign purchases of Euro-mark bonds was reflected not in the long-term capital account but in the short-term. The latter was also strengthened by swap transactions which ultimately matched German purchases of Euro-mark bonds.

Examples of the purely statistical short-term capital inflows created include German banks increasing their foreign borrowing to accommodate domestic borrowers shifting to fixed-rate borrowing via a currency swap (borrowing dollars, say, and entering into a mark–dollar currency swap as a payer of fixed-rate marks, receiver of floating-rate dollars); or German banks themselves arbitraging between the mark–dollar currency swap market (where supply was boosted by arbitragers in the Euro-mark new issue market) and the mark interest-rate swap market (where German domestic borrowers could be attracted as fixed-rate payers) by borrowing floating-rate dollars and lending floating-rate marks; or outside the swap area German corporations lending less to their foreign subsidiaries (the counterpart to these financing themselves directly via issues in the Euro-Deutschmark bond market).

The German short-term capital account has usually been in considerable underlying deficit since the emergence of the giant surplus on current account (1985–6), with the arbitrage transactions described causing the visible size of the deficit to be somewhat less. By contrast, the Japanese short-term capital account has typically been in large underlying surplus (reflecting the role of the Japanese banks in providing forward exchange cover to Japanese investors in foreign – mainly dollar – bonds; they match in large part their forward sale of yen against dollars to investors by borrowing dollars in the offshore money market and lending yen). Swap transactions in yen associated with long-term international investment and borrowing have sometimes contributed to a statistical understatement of the short-term capital inflow.

For example, the issue of convertible bonds (or bonds with warrants attached) in the Euro-dollar and foreign Swiss franc markets has been a popular form of finance with Japanese corporations. Often they have sought to swap the resulting foreign currency liability into fixed-rate yen. Sometimes the counterparties have been Japanese banks on their own account taking advantage of the arbitrage opportunity of matching a long-term forward sale of yen by becoming (in a swap) a receiver of fixed-rate yen and payer of dollars rather than by borrowing offshore.

Hence the issue of foreign currency bonds abroad simultaneously swapped into yen – from an economic standpoint a fairly neutral pair of events in determining the force of capital flow into or out of Japan (except to the extent of any unhedged conversion premium) – can have a major statistical impact on the composition of the capital account, in particular its division between long-term and short-term balances. Long-term capital imports would be bloated (under the heading of external bond issues by Japanese borrowers sold to non-Japanese investors) and short-term inflows curtailed. Analysts of foreign exchange trends would make a mistake if they interpreted the shrinking of short-term inflows as indicative of changed short-term speculative expectations (for example, Japanese investors hedging less of their dollar bond portfolios in the belief that a dollar rally is in sight) rather than as a purely statistical counterpart to that portion of external bond issues swapped into yen (the assumption being that this swap is carried out as part of a long-term rather than a short-term trading strategy).

Sometimes the counterpart to the swaps (by the Japanese issuers of foreign currency bonds) has been foreign (non-Japanese) issuers of Euro-yen bonds. Most of the foreign issues in the Euro-yen market have been driven by arbitrage profit involving the swap market, the prime-rated foreign borrower ending up with cheap finance in another currency. In so far as the foreign Euro-yen bonds are bought by foreigners they do not enter into the balance of payments; rather they are proxied (in this example) by external bond issues made by Japanese corporations. The portion bought by Japanese investors appears as a long-term capital export (under the heading of portfolio flows). Thus a bare reading of the statistics would fail to reveal the economically meaningful demand for yen bonds from international investors; on the other hand, the analyst could be encouraged to set off on the false trail of explaining an autonomous upturn in Japanese demand for Euro-yen rather than domestic bonds.

At times Japanese corporations have targeted dollar-denominated bonds directly at Japanese investors. Such transactions, being simply between residents, do not appear directly in the balance of payments. Yet their omission (totally correct according to statistical procedure) can set the analyst of capital flows on the wrong path, especially in the usual case of the borrower having swapped the dollar issue into yen. The combination of the Japanese corporation deciding to issue a dollar bond on a swapped basis (swapping into yen) and the Japanese investor seeking to purchase a dollar-denominated bond creates a force driving capital export. Yet in the statistics this force will most likely find misleading expression either in short-term capital outflows (banks acting as swap counterpart in the accommodation of demand for forward yen, thereby borrowing less offshore) or in the simultaneous omission (statistically correct) of the economically meaningful purchase from abroad of Euro-yen issues by foreign borrowers (the alternative counterpart to the swap).

Notes

Chapter 1. The market place

1. See Price (1985): 23–35.
2. For a discussion of the traditional foreign exchange swap and its key role in arbitrage relationships, see Brown (1983), chapter 2.
3. ibid., chapter 3.
4. A breakdown of transactions in the US interest-rate swap market, with some survey data, can be found in Felgran (1987).
5. See, for example, *International Financing Review*, 8 October 1988. US savings and loan associations were cited as one counterparty to Italy's swapping a jumbo fixed-rate issue into floating-rate funds.
6. Early calls were common in the Swiss franc bond market by foreign borrowers in the late 1970s and were one factor in the strong rise of the franc at that time. See Brown (1988): 363–4.
7. See Brown (1979b: 105–12) for a categorization of markets according to how liquidity is created.

Chapter 2. Arbitrage statics

1. For a description of the early literature, particularly that in German, see Einzig (1975).
2. An early statement of the theorem came in Keynes (1923).
3. See Einzig (1975).
4. See Aliber (1973), Brown (1983b: part 2; 1979a).
5. For an analogous concept of dominance in the case of covered interest arbitrage see Brown (1983a).
6. See *International Financing Review*, 23 July 1988.

Chapter 3. Arbitrage dynamics

1. See Evans (1988): 135–8.
2. See Brown (1988): 418–20.

3. See various issues of the *International Financing Review* at this time. Briefly, there was a sudden re-rating of hitherto popular perpetual floating-rate notes (no maturity date) issued by banks.
4. See Ernst (1988).
5. See Bank of Japan (1988).

Chapter 4. International capital flows

1. Some of the implications for economic policy are described in Bank for International Settlements (1986).
2. For the identity of forward exchange transactions with simultaneous borrowing and lending, see Brown (1983b): chapter 3.
3. See, for example, Brown (1978): chapter 4.
4. See Brown (1988): 382–3.
5. For examples see Brown (1983b): chapter 7.
6. It was not until January 1989 that they (foreign borrowers) could be certain that swaps were exempt from withholding tax. On 25 January the German authorities made a formal ruling; see *International Financing Review*, 28 January 1989, p. 54.

References

Aliber, R.Z. (1973) 'The interest rate parity theorem: a
reinterpretation', *Journal of Political Economy* 4: 1451-9.
Bank for International Settlements (1986) *Recent Innovations in
International Banking*, Basel: Bank for International Settlements.
Bank of Japan (1988) *Recent Developments in the Long-term Bond
Market*, Special Paper No. 170, December, Tokyo: Bank of Japan.
Brown, B. D. (1978) *Money, Hard and Soft*, London: Macmillan.
—— (1979a) 'A clarification of the interest rate parity theorem',
European Economic Review 12: 2079-87.
—— (1979b) *The Dollar–Mark Axis*, London: Macmillan.
—— (1983a) 'The swap market and its relation to currency forward
and futures markets', in M. E. Streit (ed.), *Futures Markets*, Oxford:
Blackwell.
—— (1983b) *The Forward Market in Foreign Exchange*, London:
Croom Helm.
—— (1988)*The Flight of International Capital*, London: Routledge.
Einzig, P. (1975) *A Dynamic Theory of Forward Exchange*, London:
Macmillan.
Ernst, U. (1988) 'Wie weiter mit der beruflichen Vorsorge', Zurich:
Bank Vontobel.
Evans, E. (1988) 'What drives interest rate swap spreads', in G. Parente
(ed.), *Inside the Swap Market*, London: IFR Publishing.
Felgran, F. D. (1987) 'Interest rate swaps: use, risk and prices', *New
England Economic Review*, November–December, 6: 22-3.
Keynes, J. M. (1923) *A Tract on Monetary Reform*, London:
Macmillan.
Price, J. (1985) 'The development of the swap market', in *Swap
Financing Techniques*, London: Euromoney Publications.

Index

arbitrage: arithmetic examples
36–8, 53–6; between Bunds and
euro-DMs 74–5, 104–5;
between commercial paper and
floating rate notes 41–2;
between currency and interest
rate swaps 13, 39; between euro
and domestic markets 99;
between floating rate notes and
swaps 29–32; between forward
exchange and swaps 29–32, 5,
6, 15, 21; between new issue
market and swaps 13, 39;
dominant 31, 48; intra-band
50–2; linear 40; lower cost, in
swaps 50–3; one-way 31, 33,
38; opportunity created by
withholding tax 100–1;
triangular 40; two-way 32, 50;
see also tax arbitrage
asset swap: *see also* floating rate
notes 9–10, 12, 13, 31–2;
creating synthetic Deutschmarks
91; how can add to the liquidity
of bond market 10; in Italian
ECU issues 70–1
Australian dollar:
internationalization of by swaps
95; swaps in 26

banks: *see also* Swiss, US,
German, investment, their role
in swap market 7, 15, 17–20,

22, 61; synergy between
investment and commercial 23
bank crisis: as factor in swap
origins 25
basis swap: *see* LIBOR–LIBOR
swap
Belgian–Luxembourg franc: swap
market in 77
British pound: swap market in 81;
demand for foreign bonds in
106
brokers: in swaps 17, 22
building societies: as issuers of
floating rate notes 65
Bundesbank: early restrictions on
swaps 87

Canadian dollar: swap market in
97
capital flows: *see* statistics
commercial paper market 41;
arbitrage with floating rate notes
41–2
computer: use in swap markets
27
Crash of 1987: influence on swaps
27, 105
currency substitution: promoted by
swaps 84–90
currency swap: illustrated 2, 4–5,
13; supply and demand in
13–17; vehicle for speculation
17

113

For Product Safety Concerns and Information please contact our EU representative GPSR@taylorandfrancis.com Taylor & Francis Verlag GmbH, Kaufingerstraße 24, 80331 München, Germany

Printed and bound by CPI Group (UK) Ltd, Croydon, CR0 4YY

08/05/2025

01864457-0005